"With traditional career doors slamming shut, it's easy to panic, but Chris Guillebeau sees opportunities everywhere. **Making a career out of your passion sounds like a dream, but in this straight-forward, engaging book he shows you how to get it done, one simple step at a time.**"

—Alan Paul, author of *Big in China*

"Business, like traveling, is often improved by starting poor. You are forced to improvise, innovate, and stay close to reality. You can't buy solutions, so you have to create your own. Suddenly you have the first part of success—something of value. I got all this from *The $100 Startup*, which is **full of practical advice about inventing your own livelihood.** I've done a handful of $100 startups myself, several of which I later sold. **Chris Guillebeau knows what he is talking about. Listen to this book!**"

—Kevin Kelly, author of *What Technology Wants*

"**This book is more than a 'how to' guide, it's a 'how they did it' guide that should persuade anyone thinking about starting a business that they don't need a fortune to make one.**"

—John Jantsch, author of *Duct Tape Marketing* and *The Referral Engine*

"Is that giant knot in your stomach keeping you from starting your own business or pursuing the career of your dreams? **Chris Guillebeau's seasoned, practical advice and his efficient blueprint for entrepreneurial success will alleviate your anxieties and get you on the path to being responsible for—and in control of—your future.**"

—Erin Doland, editor-in-chief of Unclutterer.com and author of *Unclutter Your Life in One Week*

"You can't grow a thriving business on wishes and dreams. You need the kind of nuts-and-bolts wisdom that only comes from hard-earned experience. **Chris Guillebeau has been in the trenches for years, and in *The $100 Startup* he guides you step-by-step through how he and dozens of others have turned their passions into profits. It's essential reading for the solopreneur!**"

—Todd Henry, author of *The Accidental Creative*

"Starting your own business doesn't have to be expensive or difficult. **Follow Chris's advice, and you'll help people, have fun, and never work for 'the man' again.**"

—Josh Kaufman, author of *The Personal MBA: Master the Art of Business*

THE $100 STARTUP

THE $100 STARTUP

**Reinvent the Way You Make a Living,
Do What You Love,
and Create a New Future**

• • •

Chris Guillebeau

CROWN
BUSINESS
NEW YORK

Published in the United States by Crown Business, an imprint of the Crown Publishing Group, a division of Random House, Inc., New York.

www.crownpublishing.com

CROWN BUSINESS is a trademark and CROWN and the Rising Sun colophon are registered trademarks of Random House, Inc.

Crown Business books are available at special discounts for bulk purchases for sales promotions or corporate use. Special editions, including personalized covers, excerpts of existing books, or books with corporate logos, can be created in large quantities for special needs. For more information, contact Premium Sales at (212) 572-2232 or e-mail specialmarkets@randomhouse.com.

Library of Congress Cataloging-in-Publication Data

Guillebeau, Chris.
The $100 startup : reinvent the way you make a living, do what you love, and create a new future / by Chris Guillebeau.
p.   cm.
1. New business enterprises—Management.   2. Entrepreneurship.   I. Title.
II. Title: One hundred dollar startup.

HD62.5.G854 2012
658.1'1—dc23   2012003093

ISBN 978-0-307-95152-6
eISBN 978-0-307-95154-0

Printed in the United States of America

Book design: Helene Berinsky
Illustrations: Mike Rohde
Jacket design: Michael Nagin
Jacket photography: Comstock/Getty Images

14 16 18 20 19 17 15 13

First Edition

This book is for:
those who take action
and
those who provide the inspiration

ROAD MAP

THE $100 STARTUP

PROLOGUE
Manifesto

A SHORT GUIDE TO EVERYTHING YOU WANT

Imagine a life where all your time is spent on the things you want to do.

Imagine giving your greatest attention to a project you create yourself, instead of working as a cog in a machine that exists to make other people rich.

Imagine handing a letter to your boss that reads, "Dear Boss, I'm writing to let you know that your services are no longer required. Thanks for everything, but I'll be doing things my own way now."

Imagine that today is your final day of working for anyone other than yourself. What if—very soon, not in some distant, undefined future—you prepare for work by firing up a laptop in your home office, walking into a storefront you've opened, phoning a client who trusts you for helpful advice, or otherwise doing what *you* want instead of what someone tells you to do?

All over the world, and in many different ways, thousands of people are doing exactly that. They are rewriting the rules of work, becoming their own bosses, and creating a new future.

This new model of doing business is well under way for these unexpected entrepreneurs, most of whom have never thought of themselves as businessmen and businesswomen. It's a *microbusiness* revolution—a way of earning a good living while crafting a life of independence and purpose.

Other books chronicle the rise of Internet startups, complete with rants about venture capital and tales of in-house organic restaurants. Other guides tell you how to write eighty-page business plans that no one will ever read and that don't resemble how an actual business operates anyway.

This book is different, and it has two key themes: *freedom* and *value*. Freedom is what we're all looking for, and value is the way to achieve it.

Stumbling onto Freedom

More than a decade ago, I began a lifelong journey of self-employment by any means necessary. I never planned to be an entrepreneur; I just didn't want to work for someone else. From a cheap apartment in Memphis, Tennessee, I watched what other people had done and tried to reverse-engineer their success. I started by importing coffee from Jamaica, selling it online because I saw other people making money from it; I didn't have any special skills in importing, roasting, or selling. (I did, however, consume much of the product through frequent "testing.")

If I needed money, I learned to think in terms of how I could get what I needed by making something and selling it, not by cutting costs elsewhere or working for someone else. This distinction was critical, because most budgets start by looking at income and then defining the available choices. I did it differently—starting with a list of what I wanted to do, and then figuring out how to make it happen.

The income from the business didn't make me rich, but it paid the bills and brought me something much more valuable than money: freedom. I had no schedule to abide by, no time sheets to fill out, no useless reports to hand in, no office politics, and not even any mandatory meetings to attend.

I spent some of my time learning how a real business works, but I didn't let it interfere with a busy schedule of reading in cafés during the day and freelancing as a jazz musician at night.

Looking for a way to contribute something greater to the world, I moved to West Africa and spent four years volunteering with a medical charity, driving Land Rovers packed with supplies to clinics throughout Sierra Leone and Liberia. I learned how freedom is connected to responsibility, and how I could combine my desire for independence with something that helped the rest of the world.

After returning to the United States, I developed a career as a writer in the same way I learned to do everything else: starting with an idea, then figuring everything else out along the way. I began a journey to visit every country in the world, traveling to twenty countries a year and operating my business wherever I went. At each step along the way, the value of freedom has been a constant compass.

There's no rehab program for being addicted to freedom. Once you've seen what it's like on the other side, good luck trying to follow someone else's rules ever again.

The Value Doctrine

The second part of this book is about *value*, a word that is often used but rarely analyzed. As we'll consider it, value is created when a person makes something useful and shares it with the world. The people whose stories you'll read in this book have succeeded because of the value they've created. Often, the combination of freedom and value comes about when someone takes action on something he or she loves to do anyway: a hobby, skill, or passion that that person ends up transforming into a business model.

The microbusiness revolution is happening all around us as people say "thanks but no thanks" to traditional work, choosing to chart their own course and create their own future. Small businesses aren't new, but never before have so many possibilities come together in the right place at the right time. Access to technology has increased greatly, and costs have gone down greatly. You can test-market your idea instantly, without waiting for months to gauge how prospects will respond to an offer. You can open a PayPal account in five minutes and receive funds from buyers in more than 180 countries.

Even better, as you build a community of loyal customers, you'll know well in advance what to make for them and how likely you are to be successful without investing a lot of money. In fact, the more you understand how your skills and knowledge can be useful to others, the more your odds of success will go up.

Perhaps most important, the vital career question of what is risky and what is safe has changed permanently. The old choice was to work at a job or take a big risk going out on your own. The new reality is that working at a job may be the far riskier choice. Instead, take the safe road and go out on your own.

What if you could achieve your own life of freedom by bypassing everything you thought was a prerequisite? Instead of borrowing money, you just start—right now—*without* a lot of money. Instead of hiring employees, you begin a project by yourself, based on your specific personal combination of passion and skill. Instead of going to business school (which doesn't actually train people to operate a small business), you save the $60,000 in tuition and learn as you go.

Remember, this book isn't about founding a big Internet startup, and it isn't about opening a traditional business by putting on a suit and begging for money at the bank. Instead, it's the account of people who found a way to live their dreams and make a good living from something they cared deeply about. What if their success could be replicated? What if there was a master plan you could follow, learning from those who have made it happen?

It's a Blueprint, Not a Vague Series of Ideas

I'll share more of my own story as we go along, but this book isn't about me—it's about other people who have found freedom, and how you can do the same thing. During an unconventional book tour, I traveled to sixty-three cities in the United States and Canada (and eventually more than fifteen additional countries), meeting with people who had made the switch from working for The Man to working for themselves.

I then worked with a small team to create a comprehensive, multiyear study involving more than a hundred interview subjects. Combing through reams of data (more than four thousand pages of written survey answers in addition to hundreds of phone calls, Skype sessions, and back-and-forth emails), I compiled the most important lessons, which are offered here for your review and action. This blueprint to freedom is fully customizable and highly actionable. At many points along the way, you'll have a chance to pause and work on your own plan before continuing to learn more about what other people have done.

A few of the people in the study are natural-born renegades, determined to go it alone from young adulthood onward, but most are ordinary people who had no intention of working on their own until later in life. Several had been laid off or fired from a job and suddenly had to find a way to pay the bills or support a family. (In almost all these cases, they said something like, "Losing my job was the best thing that ever happened to me. If I hadn't been pushed, I never would have made the leap.")

Make no mistake: The blueprint does not tell you how to do less work; it tells you how to do *better* work. The goal isn't to get rich quickly but to build something that other people will value enough to pay for. You're not just creating a job for yourself; you're crafting a legacy.

This blueprint does not involve secrets, shortcuts, or gimmicks. There are no visualization exercises here. If you think you can manifest your way to money simply by thinking about it, put this book down and spend your time doing that. Instead, this book is all about practical things you can do to take responsibility for your own future. Read it if you want to build something beautiful on the road to freedom.

Can you transition to a meaningful life oriented toward something you love to do? Yes. Can you make money doing it? Yes, and here are the stories of people who have led the way. Is there a path you can follow for your own escape plan? Yes—here is the path. Follow it to create the freedom you crave.

PART I

UNEXPECTED ENTREPRENEURS

1 • Renaissance

"The need for change bulldozed a road
down the center of my mind."

—MAYA ANGELOU

On the Monday morning of May 4, 2009, Michael Hanna put on a Nordstrom suit with a colorful tie and headed to his office building in downtown Portland, Oregon. A twenty-five-year veteran sales professional, Michael spent his days attending meetings, pitching clients, and constantly responding to email.

Arriving at work, he settled into his cubicle, reading the news and checking a few emails. One of the messages was from his boss, asking to see him later that day. The morning passed uneventfully: more emails, phone calls, and planning for a big pitch. Michael took a client out to lunch, stopping off for an espresso recharge on the way back in. He returned in time to fire off a few more replies and head to the boss's office.

Inside the office, Michael took a seat and noticed that his boss didn't make eye contact. "After that," he says, "everything happened in slow motion. I had heard story after story of this experience from other people, but I was always disconnected from it. I never thought it could happen to me."

His boss mentioned the downturn in the economy, the unavoidable need to lose good people, and so on. An H.R. manager appeared out of nowhere, walking Michael to his desk and handing him a cardboard box—*an actual box!*—to pack up his things. Michael wasn't sure what to say, but he tried to put on a brave face for his nearby colleagues. He drove home at two-thirty, thinking about how to tell his wife, Mary Ruth, and their two children that he no longer had a job.

After the shock wore off, Michael settled into an unfamiliar routine, collecting unemployment checks and hunting for job leads. The search was tough. He was highly qualified, but so were plenty of other people out pounding the pavement every day. The industry was changing, and it was far from certain that Michael could return to a well-paying job at the same level he had worked before.

One day, a friend who owned a furniture store mentioned that he had a truckload of closeout mattresses and no use for them. "You could probably sell these things one at a time on Craigslist and do pretty well," he told Michael. The idea sounded crazy, but nothing was happening on the job front. Michael figured if nothing else, he could at least sell the mattresses at cost. He called Mary Ruth: "Honey, it's a long story, but is it OK if I buy a bunch of mattresses?"

The next step was to find a location to stash the goods. Hunting around the city, Michael found a car dealership that had gone out of business recently. Times were hard in the real estate business too, so when Michael called the landlord to see if he could set up shop inside the old showroom, he had a deal. The first inventory went quickly through Craigslist and word of mouth, and the biggest problem was answering questions from potential customers about what kind of mattress they should buy. "I had no business plan and no knowledge of mattresses," Michael said. "My impression of mattress stores was that they were seedy, high-pressure places. I wasn't sure what kind of place I was trying to build, but I knew it had to be a welcoming environment where customers weren't hassled."

After the first experience went well, Michael took the plunge and studied up on mattresses, talking to local suppliers and negotiating with the landlord to remain in the former car showroom. Mary Ruth built a website. The concept of a no-hard-sell mattress store went over well in Portland, and business grew when the store offered the industry's first-ever mattress delivery *by bicycle*. (A friend built a custom tandem bike with a platform on the back that could hold a king-size mattress.) Customers who rode their own bikes to the store received free delivery, a pricing tactic that inspired loyalty and a number of fan videos uploaded to YouTube.

It wasn't what Michael had ever expected to do, but he had built a real business, profitable right from the first truckload of mattresses and providing enough money to support his family. On the two-year anniversary of his abrupt departure from corporate life, Michael was looking through his closet when he spotted the Nordstrom suit he had worn on his last day. Over the last two years, he hadn't worn it—or any other professional dress clothes—a single time. He carried the suit out to his bike, dropped it off at Goodwill, and continued on to the mattress store. "It's been an amazing two years since I lost my job," he says now. "I went from corporate guy to mattress deliveryman, and I've never been happier."

• • •

Across town from Michael's accidental mattress shop, first-time entrepreneur Sarah Young was opening a yarn store around the same time. When asked why she took the plunge at the height of the economic downturn and with no experience running a business,

Sarah said: "It's not that I had no experience; I just had a different kind of experience. I wasn't an entrepreneur before, but I was a shopper. I knew what I wanted, and it didn't exist, so I built it." Sarah's yarn store, profiled further in Chapter 11, was profitable within six months and has inspired an international following.

Meanwhile, elsewhere around the world, others were skipping the part about having an actual storefront, opening Internet-based businesses at almost zero startup cost. In England, Susannah Conway started teaching photography classes for fun and got the surprise of her life when she made more money than she did as a journalist. (Question: "What did you not foresee when starting up?" Answer: "I didn't know I was starting up!")

Benny Lewis graduated from a university in Ireland with an engineering degree, but never put it to use. Instead he found a way to make a living as a "professional language hacker," traveling the world and helping students quickly learn to speak other languages. (Question: "Is there anything else we should know about your business?" Answer: "Yes. Stop calling it a business! I'm having the time of my life.")

Welcome to the strange new world of micro-entrepreneurship. In this world, operating independently from much of the other business news you hear about, Indian bloggers make $200,000 a year. Roaming, independent publishers operate from Buenos Aires and Bangkok. Product launches from one-man or one-woman businesses bring in $100,000 in a single day, causing nervous bank managers to shut down the accounts because they don't understand what's happening.

Oddly, many of these unusual businesses thrive by giving things away, recruiting a legion of fans and followers who support their paid work whenever it is finally offered. "My marketing plan is strategic giving," said Megan Hunt, who makes hand-crafted dresses and wedding accessories in Omaha, Nebraska, shipping them all over the world. "Empowering others is our greatest marketing effort," said Scott Meyer from South Dakota. "We host training sessions, give away free materials, and answer any question someone emails to us at no charge whatsoever."

• • •

In some ways, renegade entrepreneurs who buck the system and go it alone are nothing new. *Microbusinesses*—businesses typically run by only one person—have been around since the beginning of commerce. Merchants roamed the streets of ancient Athens and Rome, hawking their wares. In many parts of rural Africa and Asia, much commerce still takes place through small transactions and barter.

Unconventional approaches to marketing and public relations have also been around for a while. Long before it was common, a band had an idea for communicating directly with fans, bypassing the traditional structure of record labels as much as possible. The fans felt like they were part of a community instead of just a crowd of adoring listeners. Oh, and instead of relying primarily on album sales for income, the band would rely on ticket sales and merchandising at an unending series of live concerts. The example sounds like it's happening today, but the year was 1967, and the band was the Grateful Dead.

What's new, however, is how quickly someone can start a business and reach a group of customers. The building process is much faster and cheaper today than it has ever been. Going from idea to startup can now take less than a month and cost less than $100—just ask any of the people whose stories you'll read in this book. Commerce may have been around forever, but scale, reach, and connection have changed dramatically. The handyman who does odd jobs and repairs used to put up flyers at the grocery store; now he advertises through Google to people searching for "kitchen cabinet installation" in their city.

It's not an elitist club; it's a middle-class, leaderless movement. All around the world, ordinary people are opting out of traditional employment and making their own way. Instead of fighting the system, they're creating their own form of work—usually without much training, and almost always without much money. These unexpected entrepreneurs have turned their passion into profit while creating a more meaningful life for themselves.

What if you could do this too? What if you could have the same freedom to set your own schedule and determine your own priorities? Good news: Freedom is possible. More good news: Freedom isn't something to be envisioned in the vaguely distant future—the future is *now*.

The $100 Startup Model

I've been hearing stories about unconventional businesses for at least a decade, even as I've been operating a series of them myself. Through my work as a writer and entrepreneur, I had access to a wide circle of microbusiness case studies: profitable businesses typically run solely by one person without much in the way of startup capital. In preparing for a comprehensive study, I began by checking with many of my friends and colleagues, but I didn't stop there.

In 2010 I produced a series of workshops on low-budget business ideas with Pamela Slim, author of *Escape from Cubicle Nation*. The first time we announced a workshop, it sold out in ninety minutes. We then offered spots in another workshop that wouldn't be held for several months, and it sold out before lunchtime. Since it was clear we had found a demand for this information, I dug deeper.

While hosting the workshops, I became interested in the

"follow-your-passion" model—the idea that successful small businesses are often built on the pursuit of a personal hobby or interest. I conducted interviews with entrepreneurs all over the world and documented their stories for an online course called the *Empire Building Kit*. The course was the inspiration for launching the project on a wider scale and then for writing this book.

I had a number of case studies in mind at the outset, but in preparation for writing the book, I cast the net much wider. I drew respondents from online and offline, collecting data through a Google form that grew to thousands of data points. As I traveled to sixty-three cities in North America on a book tour, I kept meeting and hearing about more unconventional, accidental entrepreneurs.

When I finally closed the nomination process, I had more than 1,500 respondents to choose from. All of the respondents met at least four of the following six criteria:

- **Follow-your-passion model.** Many people are interested in building a business that is based on a hobby or activity they are especially enthusiastic about. As we'll see, not every passion leads to big bank deposits, but some certainly do.

- **Low startup cost.** I was interested in businesses that required less than $1,000 in startup capital, especially those that cost almost nothing (less than $100) to begin.

- **At least $50,000 a year in net income.** I wanted profitable businesses that earned at least as much as the average North American income. As we go along, you'll notice that the range varies considerably, with many businesses earning healthy six-figure incomes or higher, but a baseline profitability level of at least $50,000 a year was required.

- **No special skills.** Since we were looking at ordinary people who created a successful business, I had a bias toward businesses that anyone can operate. This point can be hard to define, but there's a key distinction: Many businesses require specialized skills of some kind, but they are skills that can be acquired through a short period of training or independent study. You could learn to be a coffee roaster on the job, for example, but hopefully not a dentist.

- **Full financial disclosure.** Respondents for the study agreed to disclose their income projection for the current year and actual income for at least the previous two years. Furthermore, they had to be willing to discuss income and expenses in specific terms.

- **Fewer than five employees.** For the most part, I was interested in unexpected or accidental entrepreneurs who deliberately chose to remain small. Many of the case studies are from businesses operated strictly by one person, which closely relates to the goal of personal freedom that so many respondents identified.

I excluded businesses that were in "adult" or quasi-legal markets, and in most cases also excluded businesses that were highly technical or required special skills to operate. The baseline test was, "Could you explain what you do to your grandmother, and would you be willing to?"

Next, I wanted to look at businesses started by people all over the world. About half of our stories come from the United States, and half come from the rest of the world. From Silicon Valley to Atlanta, the U.S. is a hub for entrepreneurship, both in terms of values and ease of startup. But as we'll see, people from all over the world are creating their own microbusinesses, sometimes following the U.S. model and other times doing it independently.

Finally, in making the last selections for the studies presented here, I had a bias toward "interesting" stories. Not every business needs to be sexy or trendworthy—in fact, many of the ones here aren't—but I liked stories that highlighted originality and creativity. Two years ago in Minneapolis, Lisa Sellman attracted my attention by telling me about her dog care business. At first, I didn't think much of it. How profitable could a dog care business be? But then Lisa told me how much money she made: $88,000 the previous year and on track to clear six figures the next. All of a sudden I was interested. How did Lisa do it . . . and what lessons could we learn from her?

Each case study subject completed several detailed surveys about his or her business, including financial data and demographics, in addition to dozens of open-ended questions. The group surveys were followed up with further individual questions in hundreds of emails, phone calls, Skype video calls, and in-person meetings in fifteen cities around the world. My goal was to create a narrative by finding common themes among a diverse group. The collected data would be enough for several thick books by itself, but I've tried to present only the most important information here. You can learn more about the methodology for the study, including survey data and specific interviews, at 100startup.com.

• • •

In other studies, books, and media coverage, two kinds of business models get most of the attention. Business model number one is old-school: An inventor gets an idea and persuades the bank to lend her money for a growing operation, or a company spins off a division to create another company. Most corporations traded on the stock market fit this category. Business model number two is the investment-driven startup, which is typically focused on venture capital, buyouts, advertising, and market share. The business is initiated by a founder or small group of partners, but often run by a management team, reporting to a board of directors who seek to increase the business's valuation with the goal of "going public" or being acquired.

Each of the older models has strengths, weaknesses, and various other characteristics. In both of them, there is no shortage of success and failure stories. But these models and their stories are not our concern here. While business models number one and number two have been getting all the attention, something else has been happening quietly—something completely different.

Our story is about people who start their own microbusinesses without investment, without employees, and often without much of an idea of what they're doing. They almost never have a formal business plan, and they often don't have a plan at all besides "Try this out and see what happens." More often than not, the business launches quickly, without waiting for permission from a board or manager. Market testing happens on the fly. "Are customers buying?" If the answer is yes, good. If no, what can we do differently?

Like Michael's progression from corporate guy to mattress bicyclist, many of our case studies started businesses accidentally after experiencing a hardship such as losing a job. In Massachusetts, Jessica Reagan Salzman's husband called from work to say he was coming home early—and he wouldn't be going back to the office the next day. The unexpected layoff catapulted Jessica, new mother to a three-week-old, into action. Her part-time bookkeeping "hobby" became the family's full-time income. In Pennsylvania, Tara Gentile started her business with the goal of being able to work from home while caring for her children; the business grew so quickly that her husband ended up staying home too.

Across the Atlantic, David Henzell was a director for the largest advertising agency outside London. He left in part because he was bored with the work, and in part because of a diagnosis of chronic fatigue syndrome that left him struggling with "chronic director responsibilities." In his new company, Lightbulb Design, he makes the rules. "For a while the illness managed me," he said, "but now I manage it. Lightbulb started as a way for me to make a living on my terms. It's still on my terms, but now we are kicking ass!"

The people we'll meet vary considerably in the ways they chose to structure their projects. Some eventually opted for expansion, either by hiring or building teams of "virtual assistants." Erica Cosminsky grew her transcription team to seventeen people at one point, but by working with contractors instead of hiring employees, she retained the freedom to keep things simple. The Tom Bihn luggage factory in Seattle grew to a seven-figure operation, while remaining completely independent and turning down offers to sell its line to big-box stores.

Others pursued partnerships that allowed each person to focus on what he or she was best at. Fresh out of design school and disillusioned with their entry-level jobs, Jen Adrion and Omar Noory began selling custom-made maps out of an apartment in Columbus, Ohio. Patrick McCrann and Rich Strauss were competitors who teamed up to create a community for endurance athletes. Several of our stories are about married couples or partners building a business together.

But many others chose to go it alone, with the conviction that they would find freedom by working primarily by themselves. Charlie Pabst was a successful architect with a "dream job" as a store designer for Starbucks. But the desire for autonomy overcame the comfort of the dream job and the free lattes: "One day I drove to work and realized I couldn't do it anymore, called in sick, drafted my two-week notice, and the rest is history." Charlie still works as a designer, but now he works from home for clients of his choosing.

We'll view these stories as an *ensemble*: a group of individual voices that, when considered together, comprise an original composition. In sharing how different people have set themselves free from corporate misery, the challenge is to acknowledge their courage without exaggerating their skills. Most of them aren't geniuses or natural-born entrepreneurs; they are ordinary people who made a few key decisions that changed their lives. Very few of our case studies went to business school, and more than half had no previous business experience whatsoever. Several dropped out of college, and others never went in the first place.*

In sharing these stories, the goal is to provide a blueprint for freedom, a plan you can use to apply their lessons to your own escape plan. Throughout the case studies, three lessons of micro-entrepreneurship emerge. We'll focus on these lessons in various ways throughout the book.

Lesson 1: Convergence

As we'll examine it, *convergence* represents the intersection between something you especially like to do or are good at doing (preferably both) and what other people are also interested in. The easiest way to understand convergence is to think of it as the overlapping space

---

*Jeremy Brown attended two years of technical school but left without graduating. After he founded a successful company, the school invited him back to speak to students as a "success story," not realizing that his success had come from leaving the program to go out on his own. "The speech was a little awkward," he says, "but the students liked it."

between what you care about and what other people are willing to spend money on.

Consider these circles:

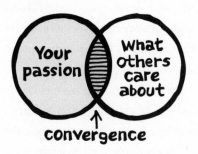

Not everything that you are passionate about or skilled in is interesting to the rest of the world, and not everything is marketable. I can be very passionate about eating pizza, but no one is going to pay me to do it. Likewise, any individual person won't be able to provide a solution to every problem or be interesting to everyone. But in the overlap between the two circles, where passion or skill meets usefulness, a microbusiness built on freedom and value can thrive.

Lesson 2: Skill Transformation

Many of the projects we'll examine were started by people with *related* skills, not necessarily the skill most used in the project. For example, teachers are usually good at more than just teaching; they're also good at things such as communication, adaptability, crowd control, lesson planning, and coordinating among different interest groups (children, parents, administrators, colleagues). Teaching is a noble career on its own, but these skills can also be put to good use in building a business.

The easiest way to understand skill transformation is to realize that you're probably good at more than one thing. Originally from Germany, Kat Alder was waitressing in London when someone said to her, "You know, you'd be really good at PR." Kat didn't know anything about PR—she wasn't even sure it stood for "public relations"—but she knew she was a good waitress, always getting good tips and making her customers happy by recommending items from the menu that she was sure they would like.

After she was let go from another temporary job at the BBC, she thought back on the conversation. She still didn't know much about the PR industry, but she landed her first client within a month and figured it out. Four years later, her firm employs five people and operates in London, Berlin, New York, and China. Kat was a great waitress and learned to apply similar "people skills" to publicizing her clients, creating a business that was more profitable, sustainable, and fun than working for someone else and endlessly repeating the list of daily specials.

Contrary to conventional wisdom, success in entrepreneurship isn't necessarily related to being the best at any particular activity. Scott Adams, the creator of the *Dilbert* comic series, explains his success this way:

> I succeeded as a cartoonist with negligible art talent, some basic writing skills, an ordinary sense of humor and a bit of experience in the business world. The "Dilbert" comic is a combination of all four skills. The world has plenty of better artists, smarter writers, funnier humorists and more experienced business people. The rare part is that each of those modest skills is collected in one person. That's how value is created.*

*Scott Adams, "How to Get a Real Education at College," *The Wall Street Journal*, April 9, 2011.

To succeed in a business project, especially one you're excited about, it helps to think carefully about all the skills you have that could be helpful to others and particularly about the combination of those skills.

Lesson 3: The Magic Formula

Bringing the first two ideas together, here is the not-so-secret recipe for microbusiness alchemy:

Passion or skill + usefulness = success

Throughout the book, we'll examine case studies by referring to this formula. Jaden Hair forged a career as the host of *Steamy Kitchen*, a cooking show and website featuring Asian cuisine. From an initial investment of $200, cookbooks, TV offers, and corporate sponsorship have all come her way due to the merging of passion and usefulness. The recipes Jaden shares with a large community on a daily basis are easy, healthy, and very popular—when I met her at an event she was hosting in Austin, I could barely get through the throngs of admirers to say hi. (Read more of Jaden's story in Chapter 2.)

Elsewhere, Brandon Pearce was a piano teacher struggling to keep up with the administrative side of his work. A programming hobbyist, he created software to help track his students, scheduling, and payment. "I did the whole project with no intention of making it into a business," he said. "But then other teachers started showing interest, and I thought maybe I could make a few extra bucks with it." The few extra bucks turned into a full-time income and more, with current income in excess of $30,000 a month. A native of Utah, Brandon now lives with his family at their second home in

Costa Rica when they aren't exploring the rest of the world. (Read more of Brandon's story in Chapter 4.)

The Road Ahead: What We'll Learn

In the quest for freedom, we'll look at the nuts and bolts of building a microbusiness through the lens of those who have done it. The basics of starting a business are very simple; you don't need an MBA (keep the $60,000 tuition), venture capital, or even a detailed plan. You just need a product or service, a group of people willing to pay for it, and a way to get paid. This can be broken down as follows:

1. Product or service: what you sell
2. People willing to pay for it: your customers
3. A way to get paid: how you'll exchange a product or service for money

If you have a group of interested people but nothing to sell, you don't have a business. If you have something to sell but no one willing to buy it, you don't have a business. In both cases, without a clear and easy way for customers to pay for what you offer, you don't have a business. Put the three together, and congratulations—you're now an entrepreneur.

These are the bare bones of any project; there's no need to overcomplicate things. But to look at it more closely, it helps to have an *offer*: a combination of product or service *plus* the messaging that makes a case to potential buyers. The initial work can be a challenge, but after the typical business gets going, you can usually take a number of steps to *ramp up* sales and income—if you want to. It helps to have a strategy of building interest and attracting attention, described here as *hustling*. Instead of just popping up one day with an offer, it helps to craft a *launch event* to get buyers excited ahead of time.

We'll look at each of these concepts in precise detail, down to dollars-and-cents figures from those who have gone before. The goal is to explain what people have done that works and closely examine how it can be replicated elsewhere. The lessons and case studies illustrate a business-creation method that has worked many times over: Build something that people want and give it to them.

There's no failproof method; in fact, failure is often the best teacher. Along the way, we'll meet an artist whose studio collapsed underneath him as he stood on the roof, frantically shoveling snow. We'll see how an adventure travel provider recovered after hearing that the South Pacific island they were taking guests to the next morning was no longer receiving visitors. Sometimes the challenge comes from too much business instead of too little: In Chicago, we'll see what happens when a business struggles under the weight of an unexpected two thousand new customers in a single day. We'll study how these and other brave entrepreneurs forged ahead and kept going, turning potential disasters into long-term successes.

• • •

The constant themes in our study are freedom and value, but the undercurrent to both is the theme of change. From his home base in Seattle, James Kirk used to build and manage computer data centers around the country. But in an act of conviction that took less than six months from idea to execution, he packed up a 2006 Mustang and left Seattle for South Carolina, on a mission to start an authentic coffee shop in the land of biscuits and iced tea. Once he made the decision, he says, all other options were closed: "There was one moment very early on when I realized, this is what I want to do, and this is what I am going to do. And that was that. Decision made. I'll figure the rest out."

As we'll see, James later got serious about making a real plan, but the more important step was the decision to proceed. Ready or not, he was heading for a major change, and it couldn't come soon enough. A few short months later, Jamestown Coffee opened for business in Lexington, South Carolina. James and his new staff had worked ten-hour days for several weeks to prepare for the opening. But there it was: a ribbon to be cut, the mayor on hand to welcome the business to the community, and a line of customers eager to sample the wares. The day had come at last, and there was no looking back.

KEY POINTS

· Microbusinesses aren't new; they've been around since the beginning of commerce. What's changed, however, is the ability to test, launch, and scale your project quickly and on the cheap.

· To start a business, you need three things: a product or service, a group of people willing to pay for it, and a way to get paid. Everything else is completely optional.

· If you're good at one thing, you're probably good at other things too. Many projects begin through a process of "skill transformation," in which you apply your knowledge to a related topic.

· Most important: merge your passion and skill with something that is useful to other people.

2 • Give Them the Fish

HOW TO PUT HAPPINESS IN A BOX AND SELL IT.

"Catch a man a fish, and you can sell it to him.
Teach a man to fish, and you ruin
a wonderful business opportunity."
—KARL MARX

Along with some of the other stories mentioned briefly in Chapter 1, we'll return to the Jamestown Coffee Company as we go along. But first, let's consider a key principle of building your way to freedom through a *microbusiness* based on a skill, hobby, or passion. The hard way to start a business is to fumble along, uncertain whether your big idea will resonate with customers. The easy way is to find out what people want and then find a way to give it to them.

Another way to consider it is to think about fish.

Picture this scenario: It's Friday night, and you head out to a nice restaurant after a long week of work. While you're relaxing over a glass of wine, the waiter comes over and informs you of the special. "We have a delicious salmon risotto tonight," he says. "That sounds perfect," you think, so you order the dish. The waiter jots it down and heads back toward the kitchen as you continue your wine and conversation.

So far, so good, right? But then the chef comes out and walks over to your table. "I understand you've ordered the salmon risotto," she says as you nod in affirmation. "Well, risotto is a bit tricky, and it's important we get the salmon right, too . . . Have you ever made it before?" Before you can respond, the chef turns around. "Tell you what, I'll go ahead and get the olive oil started. . . . You wash up and meet me back in the kitchen."

I'm guessing this experience has never happened to you, and I'm also guessing that you probably wouldn't enjoy it if it did. After getting past the initial surprise (Does the chef really want me to come back into the kitchen and help prepare the food?), you'd probably find it very odd. You know that the food in the restaurant costs much more than it would in the grocery store—you're paying a big premium for atmosphere and service. If you wanted to make salmon risotto yourself, you would have done so. You didn't go to the restaurant to learn to make a new dish; you went to relax and have people do everything for you.

What does this scenario have to do with starting a microbusiness and plotting a course toward freedom? Here's the problem: Many businesses are modeled on the idea that customers should come back to the kitchen and make their own dinner. Instead of giving people what they really want, the business owners have the idea that it's better to involve customers behind the scenes . . . because that's what they *think* customers want.

It's all the fault of the old saying: "Give a man a fish and he'll eat for a day. Teach a man to fish and he'll eat for a lifetime." This might be a good idea for hungry fishermen, but it's usually a terrible idea in business. Most customers don't want to learn how to fish. We work all week and go to the restaurant so that someone can take care of everything for us. We don't need to know the details of what goes on in the kitchen; in fact, we may not even *want* to know the details.

A better way is to give people what they actually want, and the way to do that lies in understanding something very simple about who we are. Get this point right, and a lot of other things become much easier.

• • •

For fifteen years, John and Barbara Varian were furniture builders, living on a ranch in Parkfield, California, a tiny town where the welcome sign reads "Population 18." The idea for a side business came about by accident after a group of horseback riding enthusiasts asked if they could pay a fee to ride on the ranch. They would need to eat, too—could John and Barbara do something about that? Yes, they could.

In the fall of 2006, a devastating fire burned down most of their inventory, causing them to reevaluate the whole operation. Instead of rebuilding the furniture business (no pun intended), they decided to change course. "We had always loved horses," Barbara said, "so we decided to see about having more groups pay to come to the ranch." They built a bunkhouse and upgraded other buildings, putting together specific packages for riding groups that included all meals and activities. John and Barbara reopened as the V6 Ranch, situated on 20,000 acres exactly halfway between Los Angeles and San Francisco.

Barbara's story stood out to me because of something she said. I always ask business owners what they sell and why their customers buy from them, and the answers are often insightful in more ways than one. Many people answer the question directly—"We sell widgets, and people buy them because they need a widget"—but once in a while, I hear a more astute response.

"We're not selling horse rides," Barbara said emphatically. "We're offering freedom. Our work helps our guests escape, even if just for a moment in time, and be someone they may have never even considered before."

The difference is crucial. Most people who visit the V6 Ranch have day jobs and a limited number of vacation days. Why do they choose to visit a working ranch in a tiny town instead of jetting off to lie on a beach in Hawaii? The answer lies in the story and messaging behind John and Barbara's offer. Helping their clients "escape and be someone else" is far more valuable than offering horse rides. Above all else, the V6 Ranch is selling happiness.

• • •

On the other side of the country, Kelly Newsome was a straight-A student and an ambitious Washington, D.C., career climber. By the time she started college, she already had the goal of big career achievement in mind. From the top of her class at the University of Virginia School of Law, she went on to a high-paying job as a Manhattan lawyer—her dream for more than six years. Alas, Kelly soon discovered that dutifully checking the company's filings for compliance with the Securities Act day in and day out wasn't exactly what she had hoped for back in law school. After the high of scoring her dream job wore off and the reality of being a well-paid paper pusher set in, Kelly wanted a change.

Abandoning her $240,000-a-year corporate law gig five years in, Kelly left for a new position at Human Rights Watch, the international charity. This job was more fulfilling than the moneymaking job, but it also helped her realize that she really wanted to be on her own. Before the next change, Kelly took time off and traveled the world. Yoga had always been a passion for her, and during her time away, she underwent a two-hundred-hour training course, followed by teaching in Asia and Europe. The next step was Higher Ground Yoga, a private practice she founded back in Washington,

D.C. There were plenty of yoga studios in D.C., but Kelly wanted to focus on a specific market: busy women, usually executives, ages thirty to forty-five and often with young children or expecting. In less than a year, Kelly built the business to the $50,000+ level, and she's now on track for more than $85,000 a year.

The practice has its weaknesses—during a big East Coast "snowpocalypse," Kelly was unable to drive to her appointments for nearly three weeks, losing income for much of that time. Despite the lower salary and the problem of losing business during bad weather, Kelly says she wouldn't return to her old career. Here's how she put it: "One time when I was a lawyer, having just worked with an outstanding massage therapist, I said to her, 'It must be so great to make people so happy.' And it is." Like Barbara and John in California, Kelly discovered that the secret to a meaningful new career was directly related to making people feel good about themselves.

Where Do Ideas Come From?

As you begin to think like an entrepreneur, you'll notice that business ideas can come from anywhere. When you go to the store, pay attention to the way they display the signage. Check the prices on restaurant menus not just for your own budget but also to compare them with the prices at other places. When you see an ad, ask yourself: What is the most important message the company is trying to communicate?

While thinking like this, you'll notice opportunities for microbusiness projects everywhere you go. Here are a few common sources of inspiration.

An inefficiency in the marketplace. Ever notice when something isn't run the way it should be, or you find yourself looking for something that doesn't exist? Chances are, you're not the only one frustrated, and you're not the only one who wants that nonexistent thing.

Make what you want to buy yourself, and other people will probably want it too.

New technology or opportunity. When everyone started using smart phones, new markets cropped up for app developers, case manufacturers, and so on. But the obvious answer isn't the only one: Makers of nice journals and paper notebooks also saw an uptick in sales, perhaps in part because of customers who didn't want everything in their lives to be electronic.

A changing space. As we saw with Michael's example in Chapter 1, car dealerships were going out of business, and he was able to rent his first temporary mattress space on the cheap. Not everyone would have thought of locating a mattress shop in a former car dealership, but Michael grabbed the opportunity.

A spin-off or side project. One business idea can lead to many others. Whenever something is going well, think about offshoots, spin-offs, and side projects that could also bring in income. Brandon Pearce, whom we'll see more of in Chapter 4, founded Studio Helper as a side project to his main business of Music Teacher's Helper. It now brings in more than $100,000 a year on its own.

Tip: When thinking about different business ideas, also think about money. Get in the habit of equating "money stuff" with ideas. When brainstorming and evaluating different projects, money isn't the sole consideration—but it's an important one. Ask three questions for every idea:

a. How would I get paid with this idea?

b. How much would I get paid from this idea?

c. Is there a way I could get paid more than once?

We'll look at money issues more in Chapters 10 and 11.

What Is Value?

The stories of the V6 Ranch and Higher Ground Yoga are good examples of how freedom and value are related. In California, John and Barbara found a way to pursue the outdoor lives they wanted by inviting guests to make the ranch their escape. Meanwhile, even though Kelly makes less money (at least for now) in her new career, her health is better and she does work she enjoys—a trade-off she was happy to make. Freedom was Kelly's primary motivation in making the switch, but the key to her success is the value she provides her clients.

Let's stop for a moment and look at the concept of *value*, a word that is often used without much exploration. What is value, exactly? Here's a basic definition:

> **val-ue**: something desirable and of worth, created through exchange or effort

In our context, an even easier way to think about it is: *Value means helping people.* If you're trying to build a microbusiness and you begin your efforts by helping people, you're on the right track. When you get stuck, ask yourself: How can I give more value? Or more simply: How can I help my customers more? Freedom and value have a direct relationship: You can pursue freedom for yourself while providing value for others. As we saw in the discussion of convergence, a business ultimately succeeds because of the value it provides its end users, customers, or clients.

More than anything else, value relates to emotional needs. Many business owners talk about their work in terms of the *features* it offers, but it's much more powerful to talk about the *benefits* customers receive. A feature is descriptive; a benefit is emotional.

Consider the difference in the stories we've looked at in the chapter thus far. The V6 Ranch helps people "escape and be someone new." Isn't that more powerful than just offering a horse ride? Kelly's private classes help busy female executives prepare for their day in a quiet setting, a much more meaningful and tailor-made experience than going to the gym with hundreds of other people.

We can apply the same thinking to the examples we briefly reviewed in Chapter 1. At its most basic level, we could say that Jaden Hair (founder of Steamy Kitchen) offers recipes on her website, but plenty of websites have recipes. A much stronger benefit, and the one that Jaden puts forward, is that her work helps families spend quality time making and enjoying delicious food. Similarly, Megan Hunt makes dresses, but that's not the point: She also helps brides share in the anticipation, celebration, and memories of a perfect day. Who wouldn't pay for that? The list below provides a contrast between features and benefits.*

	Feature (Descriptive)	Benefit (Emotional)
V6 Ranch	Horse rides and campfires	Stay with us and become a cowboy (or a cowgirl)
Higher Ground Yoga	Private yoga classes for busy women	Relax and prepare for the day through a personalized, guided practice
Megan Hunt	Wedding dresses and accessories	Feel special on your big day
Steamy Kitchen	Recipes and food stories	Spend quality time with your family
Anonymous Restaurant	Food and drinks	Relax and let us take care of you at the end of a busy week

*See the "Fish Stories" appendix at the back of the book for twenty-five more examples of how to reframe a descriptive concept as a benefit-driven story.

This kind of analysis applies even to businesses that you might think of as boring or commodity-based. Michael Hanna (the mattress guy) talked with me about selling a mattress to a family with an infant and then seeing them return two years later with their three-year-old, who now needed to upgrade to her first bed. This kind of story, which Michael tries to communicate frequently, is much more interesting than talking about box springs or mattress ratings.

Overall, the more a business can focus on core benefits instead of boring features, the more customers will connect . . . and purchase. As you think about how to apply the $100 Startup model to your own quest for freedom, these three strategies will help.

Strategy I: Dig Deeper to Uncover Hidden Needs

You might think it's obvious that restaurant patrons don't want to wander back to the kitchen and make their own meals, but sometimes what people say they want and what they actually want are different things. Kyle Hepp, a wedding photographer who travels the world from her home base in Santiago, Chile, learned that sometimes you have to look deeper. Kyle's clients tend to be young and hip, and they're drawn to her work because it is non-traditional. Sometimes they even say they don't want *any* traditional wedding shots. "We're not into old-school," was how one couple put it. Kyle agrees and spends her time at the wedding getting fun, candid shots that she knows the couple will like.

But that's not all. Having done this for a while, Kyle knows that what her clients want and what they say they want may be different—and she also knows that the families of the bride and groom may have preferences of their own. Here's how she handles these competing desires:

On the day of the wedding, I'll grab them and say, "Let's get your family and just do a couple of traditional shots." I'll make it quick and painless. I make sure everyone is laughing and having a good time and it's not those awful, everybody-stare-at-the-camera-and-look-miserable kinds of shots. And then after the wedding, when I deliver those photos, either the bride and groom's parents will be thrilled to have those pictures (which in turn makes the couple happy), or the bride and groom themselves will end up saying they're so happy that we did those shots.

Kyle goes above and beyond by giving her photography clients what they really want . . . even if they hadn't realized it themselves.

Strategy 2: Make Your Customer a Hero

In India I heard from Purna Duggirala, who said that he operates a training business to "help people become awesome at Microsoft Excel." Microsoft Excel doesn't interest me much, but Purna's financial details caught my attention: In the "Last Year's Net Income" column on my survey form, he had written $136,000. A salary like that is impressive where I live, but I've traveled enough to know that in India it's huge. What's more, Purna was on track to earn more than $200,000 the next year, his third year of operation. His customers were big fans. When I Googled him, I found a comment that said he was one user's "BFF for Excel," his best friend forever. What was he doing to attract such a response from spreadsheet users?

Purna started his website several years back, but for a while it only contained posts about his family and life in India. In 2009, he settled in and got more serious, chronicling a series of tips and tutorials about using Excel to become more productive. Crucially, he didn't target Indians, but instead reached out to interested prospects all over the world. He also didn't depend on advertising revenue, something that very few people in our study mentioned. Instead, he created products and services himself, offering downloadable guides and an ongoing training school.

He was also a good copywriter. Updating spreadsheets can sound like incredibly tedious work, but Purna positioned the core benefit away from numbers and toward something far more powerful: "Our training programs make customers a hero in front of their bosses or colleagues." Not only would their work become easier, Purna said, but other people would recognize and appreciate them for simplifying a complicated process.

A former business analyst, Purna quit his job when it became apparent that he would earn much more money with the new business. Despite having such a high income in India, Purna and his wife continue to live frugally. "We are in a position where we would not have to worry about money for lots of years to come," he says. Even better, new customers arrive every day from Google searches, mainstream media coverage, and hundreds of links. "If I wanted to turn it off," he told me, "it would be very difficult." Take it from Purna: If spreadsheets can be made sexy, surely any business can find a way to communicate a similar message.

Strategy 3: Sell What People Buy

In deciding what to sell, the best approach is to *sell what people buy*—in other words, think more about what people really want than about what you think they need. Perhaps a story of my own failure-to-success progression will help illustrate this principle. Early in the life of my business, I created a project called Travel Ninja. Since I've been to more than 150 countries and regularly fly more than 200,000 miles a year, I've learned a lot about getting from place to place on a budget. Travel Ninja would be a guide to illustrate how it all works—how to book round-the-world tickets, how to take advantage of airline mistake fares, and so on.

As I surveyed my audience, the initial response was encouraging. Plenty of people said they were excited and wanted to learn about these topics. A previous launch for another product had sold five hundred copies right off the bat, so on the big day I dutifully got up early and updated the site to make it live. Then I waited . . . and waited. Orders came in, but at a much slower rate than I expected. At the end of the launch day, I had sold only a hundred copies—not terrible, but not great either.

For several weeks, I was puzzled by the low response. The feedback from the customers who purchased Travel Ninja was almost unanimously positive, but so few people had purchased that I knew something was wrong with the messaging. Finally I figured it out: Most people don't care about the intricacies of how airlines work; they just want to know how to get cheap tickets. My prospects who didn't buy felt overwhelmed by the details and complexities. Like the overeager chef at the beginning of the chapter, I was trying to take them into the kitchen with me, not just giving them the meal they wanted.

Ah-ha. Lesson learned. I regrouped a year later with another travel product. This one was called Frequent Flyer Master, and I did everything I could to make it more accessible. I even used the previous experience as part of the sales copy: "Maybe you don't want to travel to twenty countries a year like I do. But if you could go to *one place* for nearly free, where would it be?"

This product did much better, selling five hundred copies on launch day and going on to produce more than $50,000 in net income over the next year. The success was also quite a relief, because for almost a year I had wondered whether people would buy information about travel. Thankfully, they will—if it's packaged properly in a way that meets their needs.

Another year later, I applied the lesson even further: The most frequent request from Frequent Flyer Master owners, who otherwise loved the product, was for more updates on late-breaking travel opportunities. With that in mind, I created the Travel Hacking Cartel to tell people exactly what to do to take advantage of deals all over the world. The careful message this time was: Don't worry about the details; just do what we say and you'll regularly earn enough miles for free plane tickets every year.

This launch did the best of all—more than three thousand customers joined on the first day. I had finally figured out how to give my customers what they wanted.

Product 1:	Product 2:	Product 3:
Travel Ninja	Frequent Flyer Master	Travel Hacking Cartel
100 Sales	500 Sales	3,000 Sales

Six Steps to Getting Started Right Now

As we saw from the stories in Chapter 1, you don't need a lot of money or special training to operate a business. You just need a product or service, a group of people who want to buy it, and a way to get paid. We'll look at each of these things in more detail throughout the book, but you don't have to wait to get started. Here are the six steps you need to take:

1. Decide on your product or service.
2. Set up a website, even a very basic one (you can get a free one from WordPress.org).
3. Develop an offer (an offer is distinct from a product or service; see Chapter 7 for help).

4. Ensure you have a way to get paid (get a free PayPal account to start).

5. Announce your offer to the world (see Chapter 9 for more on this).

6. Learn from steps 1 through 5, then repeat.

Almost all microbusiness building follows this sequence of events. Of course, we'll be discussing specifics as we go along, but it's always better to start from where you are than to wait for everything to be perfect.

If you have an existing business and are thinking about how to apply the concepts from this book, focus on either getting money in the bank or developing new products or services. These are the most important tasks of your business—not administration, maintenance, or anything else that takes time without creating wealth or value. If you're not sure what to do, think about any of these ideas:

Can you contact your customer list with a special offer or incentive?

Can you introduce a new product or service to complement your existing portfolio?

If you're a coach or consultant, can you offer a special deal for clients who prepay?

Is there a new way you can attract subscribers, clients, or customers?

But one way or another . . . just do something. Friedrich Engels said: "An ounce of action is worth a ton of theory." Choose the ounce of action today.

What People Really Want

As I learned from my early mistakes, homing in on what customers really want from a business is critical. Simply put, we want *more* of some things and *less* of others. In the "More" column are things such as love, money, acceptance, and free time. We all want more of those things, right? In the "Less" column are the undesirables: things such as stress, long commutes, and bad relationships. If your business focuses on giving people more of what they want *or* taking away something they don't want (or both), you're on the right track.

More	Less
Love	Stress
Money	Conflict
Acceptance	Hassle
Free time	Uncertainty

A spa takes away stress while making guests feel loved and accepted. A popular message is, "We'll do everything for you—relax and leave the details to us." This is also the message that a good restaurant sends, not, "Come back into the kitchen and make your own dinner."

Brooke Snow, an artist and musician, struggled to make a living by teaching classes in her small Utah town. She got by without working a real job and paid for college without going into debt, which could be considered a success on its own, but making ends meet was a continual battle. One day she realized the obvious: Instead of putting up flyers in Logan, Utah, and hoping for enough phone calls, what if she could teach anywhere in the world?

The change happened by accident, ironically after one of the worst days of her initial business. "I had to cancel a class due to underenrollment," Brooke says. "At the time my husband was starting graduate school, and we had an eight-month-old baby and a new home." Needless to say, the pressure was mounting. When she phoned Micah, one of the few students who had enrolled, to notify him of the cancellation, it turned out he was a doctoral candidate in instructional technology with an emphasis on distance education.

Brooke describes herself as a good photographer and teacher but not highly technical. Happily, she is also good at bartering—and in this case, she offered private lessons to Micah in exchange for his help in setting up an online course. Since it was almost perfectly in line with what he was studying, Micah was thrilled to help Brooke make the online transition.

In the last year Brooke taught all her classes locally, she made $30,000. In the first year she offered the class online, she made more than $60,000. Nice! Going from offline to online helped a lot, but Brooke also attributes the successful transition to something else: the idea of always being willing to share. Early in her career, she went to a seminar where she heard someone say, "If you make your business about helping others, you'll always have plenty of work." Here's what happened next:

> That statement changed my life. I was in an over-saturated market of photographers competing for portrait work, all of whom were very closed about sharing any trade secrets. I let go of fear and embraced the concept of helping others (so I could have "plenty of work"!) and decided to start teaching classes on photography in my basement. One family skeptic cautioned me that I would be "training my competition." Thankfully, making my business about helping others has proved itself over and over.

We'll return to Brooke's theme several times throughout the book. I call it the freely receive, freely give approach. When all else fails, ask yourself how you can help people more.

What do people really, *really* want? At the end of the day, they want to be happy, and businesses that help their customers be happy are well-positioned to succeed. The V6 Ranch creates modern cowboys. Kelly's yoga practice helps busy executives prepare for their day in peace. The restaurant we went to at the end of a stressful week—when it's not making its customers pop back into the kitchen—helps its patrons relax and decompress over a glass of wine and great service.

Conversations with the group returned to this theme many times in different ways. The common theme was to figure out what people want and then find a way to give it to them. This is the road map to a successful, profitable business. As you build your escape plan, keep your eyes on the prize: creating real value by giving people what they really want.

KEY POINTS

- *Value* means "helping people." Our unexpected entrepreneurs discovered that when they focused on providing value above all else, their businesses were successful.

- Give people what they really want, not just what you think they should have. Give them the fish!

- The more you can market a core benefit instead of a list of features, the easier it will be to profit from your idea. Core benefits usually relate to emotional needs more than physical needs.

- Most people want more of some things (money, love, attention) and less of other things (stress, anxiety, debt). Always focus on what you can add or take away to improve someone's life . . . and then prepare to get paid.

> **"Passion, though a bad regulator,**
> **is a powerful spring."**
> **—RALPH WALDO EMERSON**

Like many of us, Gary Leff begins his day with email. As a CFO for two university research centers in northern Virginia, he's in touch with colleagues from morning to night. It's a good job that he enjoys, and he has no plans to leave. But the "early early" morning email traffic comes from another source: Gary's part-time business as a specific kind of consultant.

Like me, Gary is an active "travel hacker," earning hundreds of thousands of frequent flyer miles every year through various airline promotions. Many executives also earn plenty of miles, usually from business credit card charges, but earning miles and redeeming them for actual vacations are two different things. The executives typically have no idea how the process works and don't have the time to learn. How many miles do you need for any specific trip? What if the airline tells you no seats are available? If you don't know what you're doing, it's easy to get frustrated and give up.

That's where Gary comes in. For a fee (currently $250 for up to two passengers with the same itinerary), Gary will set up the trip of your dreams based on preferences you select. Clients tell Gary where they want to go, which airline their miles are coming from, and any restrictions they have on their travel dates. Then Gary gets to work, combing databases to check on availability, phoning the airlines, and taking advantage of every loophole.

It may sound strange to pay $250 for something you could do on your own for free, but the value Gary provides through the service is immense: Many of the trips he arranges would otherwise cost $5,000 or more. He specializes in first- and business-class itineraries, and some of them feature as many as six airlines on a single award ticket. You want a free stopover in Paris en route to Johannesburg? No problem. You want to allow plenty of time to visit the Lufthansa first-class terminal in Frankfurt before continuing on to Singapore? Done. If he's not successful in booking your trip, you don't pay—the business succeeds only when it provides real value to clients.

In addition to executives, Gary's clients are often retirees headed for cruises and couples planning a once-in-a-lifetime trip: basically anyone who has a bunch of miles but doesn't want to go through the hassle of figuring out how to use them. Business picked up after he was featured in *Condé Nast Traveler,* but aside from calling the airlines to book the tickets, Gary manages communications entirely by email. The part-time job brought in $75,000 last year and is on track to top six figures annually. Since he has the full-time CFO gig and other business ventures, Gary invests the money instead of spending it. "I honestly do this because it's fun," he says. Meanwhile, he cashes in miles from his own bulging mileage accounts to travel the world with his wife, squeezing in luxury trips to the Philippines and Thailand between financial planning meetings back home.

• • •

Gary's business, like many others we'll look at, can be described as a follow-your-passion business. Gary was passionate about travel and had found a number of creative ways to enjoy first-class trips around the world at economy prices. He started helping people do the same thing, first as a volunteer community member for several travel forums, then on a blog, and then on an individual basis for people he knew. Word got around—"Hey, Gary, I'd like to take my wife to Europe and I have all these miles . . . What do I do?"—and before he knew it, he had more requests for help than he could handle.

The next logical step was to start charging. He built a very basic website and set up shop in a short period of time, not entirely sure what would happen next. Would anyone purchase this unusual service? Well, yes, they would—and even though Gary is content in his day job and has no plans to leave, he no longer depends on it. If something changed at work, he'd have no problem living off the funds from his side business or ramping it up to something bigger.

Gary's story is inspiring but not all that uncommon. As I foraged for case studies and went from interview to interview, I learned to stop being surprised when I heard that a coupon-clipping website run by a single mom brought in $60,000 part-time or that a handmade toy business was closing in on $250,000 and hiring multiple employees.

Instant Consultant Biz

Gary's business is great, and no one cares that his website looks like it was made ten years ago. He also didn't wait for someone to accredit or endorse him for his business. There is no "consulting school" or degree. You can start a new business as a consultant in about one day, if not sooner.

Follow these two basic rules:

1. Pick something specific as opposed to something general. Don't be a "business consultant" or a "life coach"—get specific about what you can really do for someone.

2. No one values a $15-an-hour consultant, so do not underprice your service. Since you probably won't have forty hours of billable work every week, charge at least $100 an hour or a comparable fixed rate for the benefit you provide.

OPENING FOR BUSINESS*

I will help clients _____. After hiring me, they will receive [core benefit + secondary benefit].

I will charge $xxx per hour or a flat rate of _____ per service. This rate is fair to the client and to me.

My basic website will contain these elements:

a. The core benefit that I provide for clients and what qualifies me to provide it (remember that qualifications may have nothing to do with education or certifications; Gary is qualified to book vacations with miles because he's done it for himself many times)

b. At least two stories of how others have been helped by the service (if you don't have paying clients yet, do the work for free with someone you know)

c. Pricing details (always be up front about fees; never make potential clients write or call to find out how much something costs)

d. How to hire me immediately (this should be very easy)

I will find clients through [word-of-mouth, Google, blogging, standing on the street corner, etc.].

I will have my first client on or before ___·[short deadline].

Welcome to consulting! You're now in business.

*You can create, customize, and download your own "Instant Consultant Biz" template at 100startup.com.

When I met Megan Hunt at the co-working space she owns in Omaha, it was 6 p.m. and she was just coming to work. Megan keeps odd hours, preferring to work through the night with her infant in tow. Unlike most of our stories, Megan was determined to be an entrepreneur from a young age. "I started when I was nineteen and a sophomore in college," she said. "I never intended to do anything but work for myself. I always knew that I didn't want a conventional job, so I never expected to resign myself to a fate other than the one I wanted as an artist. I worked a few eight-to-five desk jobs, but I wasn't discouraged because I only saw them as the means to an end: gaining enough capital to start my own full-time venture."

Megan now makes custom wedding dresses and bridal accessories full-time, selling them to women age twenty-four to thirty all over the world (42 percent of her customer base is international). After earning $40,000 her first year, she's now scaling up by carefully hiring two employees as well as founding the co-working space where her business is situated. (Since she's the owner, no one can complain about her night-owl work habits.)

Almost every business owner we'll meet in our journey has at least one disaster story, when something went off track or even threatened the life of the business. In Megan's case, the big disaster came right before the holiday season in 2010. After spending seventy hours crafting high-end flower kits for two customers, she shipped them out via the U.S. Postal Service . . . and the packages disappeared into the postal service void. "It was terrible," Megan told me. "I had to refund money I didn't have, and the worst part was thinking about the brides who now didn't have flowers for their wedding." But she did what she had to do—refunded money, wrote teary apology notes, posted the whole story on her blog for others to learn from—and moved on.

Aside from vowing never to use USPS again, Megan loves her business and wouldn't want to do anything differently. "I spend every day learning from people who inspire and motivate me in the co-working space," she says, "and I interact every day with customers who are in the midst of their own love stories. I have a young daughter who I am able to bring to work. My earning potential is unlimited, and I am free to reinvest in my happiness with every dollar that comes in."

• • •

It all sounds so simple: Pick something you love and build a business around it, the way Gary and Megan did. *Cha-ching!* But is it really that easy? As you might expect, the real answer is more complex. Building a business around a passion can be a great fit for many people, but not everyone.

In the rush to pursue a passion, a number of things tend to get left out. First, you can't pursue just any passion—there are plenty of things you may be passionate about that no one will pay you for. Remember the all-important lesson of convergence we've been looking at throughout the book. You must focus continually on how your project can help other people, and why they'll care about what you're offering in the first place. I like to eat pizza, but no matter how passionate I am, it's doubtful I could craft a career around my love for mushrooms and black olives. Instead, I had to find something more interesting to the rest of the world.

Sometimes a false start precedes a successful microbusiness. In Reno, Nevada, Mignon Fogarty created the QDT Network, best known for her signature show *Grammar Girl*. The show was a huge hit almost from the beginning, spawning a line of books, related programs, and non-stop media attention. But before she

was Grammar Girl, Mignon pursued a similar idea in an unsuccessful attempt to build popularity through podcasting. Here's
how she tells the story:

> Before I launched the successful *Grammar Girl* podcast, I was
> the host of a science podcast called *Absolute Science*. I loved
> doing that show and I was passionate about it. I actually put
> more effort into promoting that show than I did for the *Gram-
> mar Girl* podcast, and although *Absolute Science* was well
> received, after doing it for nearly a year it was clear that the
> show was never going to make enough money to make it worth
> the time required to produce it.

Mignon changed course, trading science for grammar. The
answer wasn't to abandon her passion altogether but to make sure
she connected the right passion with the right audience.

"Absolute Science"   *"Grammar Girl"*

Passion . . . but not   Passion . . . *and* a

enough audience   substantial audience

Next, many successful follow-your-passion business owners
understand an important principle that aspiring (and unsuccessful)
business owners don't. The missing piece is that you usually don't
get paid for your hobby itself; you get paid for helping other people
pursue the hobby or for something indirectly related to it. This
point is critical. I began my writing career by sharing stories about
a quest to visit every country in the world, but I don't get paid for
that. I have to create value in my business the same way anyone else
does—without real value, I wouldn't get paid, and the travel would
be just a hobby (albeit a passionate one).

Let's look at another example. Benny Lewis, originally from Ireland, likes to say he gets paid to learn languages. Benny's story is inspiring: He makes more than $65,000 a year, reports to no one, and goes from country to country immersing himself in different cultures. But as we look at the story more carefully, we find that there's more to it.

I first met Benny on a layover in Bangkok. Benny doesn't drink, which is probably a good thing because he is quite possibly the most naturally enthusiastic person I've ever met. Over a couple of mango juices, he told me his story. Twenty-four years old, Benny had been traveling abroad for the past two years. As a child, he spoke only English. He graduated with an engineering degree and no known aptitude for foreign languages. Moving to Spain after graduation and consulting with clients back home, he became determined to learn Spanish.

Six months into his stay in Seville, however, Benny felt frustrated with still not knowing the language, spending most of his time with a group of expatriates and Spaniards who spoke English. He decided to speak only Spanish for an entire month, with no exceptions. At first it was awkward and embarrassing; he didn't know how to conjugate verbs, so he just used the present tense and wildly waved his arms behind him to indicate that something had already happened. But the funny thing about using only another language is that you learn it much more quickly than when you rely on English as a backup. Within a few weeks, Benny was speaking comfortably. The month-long immersion was much better than the six months before it, and he was now hooked on learning other languages. He moved to Berlin and learned German, then to Paris to learn French, and then to Prague to learn Czech, a notoriously difficult language.

Putting his engineering career on hold, Benny started traveling and never stopped, working at short-term consulting jobs to pay the bills wherever he could. With his non-stop energy, he got up in the middle of the night for conference calls in North America. Being single (and not drinking) made it easy to live on a small amount of money, but it was obvious that Benny had a great skill to share with the world. His message to everyone who would listen—by this point the whole bar of expats had heard about it—was that anyone can learn another language even if you think you aren't "gifted" or spoke only one language as a child.

Benny's method was based on proven success. Within two years, he had learned seven languages (fluently!), and regularly tested himself with native speakers he met while traveling. Once in a while, he tutored someone in language learning, but the approach was scattershot.

"Benny, your skill is amazing," I said when I met him that night in Bangkok. "Why don't you get more serious about teaching this method to more people?" (To be fair, I can't take much credit for pushing him. Benny had been thinking about the idea for a while, and many other people had gathered around the bar at that point, encouraging him.)

He toyed with a few different names for the idea before hitting on the perfect one: Fluent in 3 Months. Everyone raised a bottle of beer in approval while Benny sipped his juice. Just as soon as he learned Thai (his *eighth* language), he would get to work outlining everything he knew about language hacking.

The vision was solid, but the work was tough. Benny struggled with fitting everything he knew into a collection of documents, videos, and interviews. He kept waiting for it to be perfect . . . and then he kept waiting. "I finally just had to give up on perfection and get the thing out the door," he said later. The course is now available in eight languages—all taught by Benny himself, naturally.

To market Fluent in 3 Months, Benny made YouTube videos giving a tour of his apartment in five languages (including different dialects). He stood on street corners in various countries and sang in the national language, dressing up in native costume and offering free hugs. When I ran into him next in Texas, he was wearing a set of goggles on top of a hat. "Uh, what's with the goggles?" I asked. His answer was typical: "I wear them when I travel so people will ask, 'Why are you wearing those?' Then I have an easy way to get to know them and try to learn their language."

Benny says he gets paid for learning languages, but as you can see, there's more to the story: He actually gets paid for helping people. True, the inspirational side is important (people enjoy watching and sharing his videos), but without the helpfulness, he would just be the sober Irishman who speaks a lot of languages and there would be no business model.

Along with first understanding that not every passion makes a good business and then realizing that businesses and hobbies are often distinct, there's one more important point: You may just not *want* to combine your hobby with your work. If the hobby or passion serves as an important stress reliever from your day job or other commitments, are you sure you want to assume full-time responsibility for your hobby? Some people find that it's better to keep their passion separate from their work.

Review the Reality Check Checklist below to see if a follow-your-passion business is a good idea for you. Benjamin Franklin, an old-school entrepreneur, put it this way: "If passion drives you, let reason hold the reins."

Reality Check Checklist

Questions for You

- Instead of just during your free time, would you enjoy pursuing your hobby at least twenty hours a week?
- Do you enjoy teaching others to practice the same hobby?
- Do you like the ins and outs (all the details) of your hobby?
- If you had to do a fair amount of administrative work related to your hobby, would you still enjoy it?

Questions for the Marketplace

- Have other people asked for your help?
- Are enough other people willing to pay to gain or otherwise benefit from your expertise?
- Are there other businesses serving this market (usually a good thing) but not in the same way you would?

Note: Chapter 6 looks at market testing in more detail. If you're not sure how to answer the marketplace questions, stay tuned.

When I asked our group of unexpected entrepreneurs about the follow-your-passion model, I frequently heard a nuanced answer. Almost no one said, "Yes! You should always follow your passion wherever it leads." Similarly, almost no one dismissed the idea out of hand. The nuance comes from the idea that passion *plus* good business sense creates an actual business.

To understand how passion can *sometimes* translate into a profitable business, look at the chart on page 52. In addition to passion, you must develop a skill that provides a solution to a problem. Only when passion merges with a skill that other people value can you truly follow your passion to the bank.

	Passion	Skill	Problem	Opportunity
Gary	International travel	Books high-value award tickets	Lack of industry transparency, perceived difficulty	Gary books award tickets for clients who lack time and knowledge
Benny	Language learning	Learns languages *and* has a proven teaching system	People want to learn languages but have failed through traditional methods	Benny breaks down the barriers and provides a solution
Megan	Handmade dresses and wedding accessories	Custom handicraft *and* builds relationships over a long period of time	Brides want something special and handcrafted	Megan supports a once-in-a-lifetime (one hopes) occasion
Mignon	Clear writing and use of the English language	Communicates grammar "rules" in a fun way	Perception that studying grammar is difficult or boring	Mignon educates her audience through stories and examples

Another way to think about it is

$$(\text{Passion} + \text{skill}) \rightarrow (\text{problem} + \text{marketplace}) = \text{opportunity}$$

Although it is important, passion is just one part of the equation. If Gary's skill at booking award tickets suddenly disappeared, it wouldn't matter how passionate he is about travel. No matter how passionate Megan is about her dresses, if a willing marketplace didn't exist that is eager to buy them, she couldn't be in business.

The next step is to transfer your passion into a business model. Everyone we've met thus far has used a slightly different business model to monetize his or her project, so let's look at how each of these four examples cashed in.

Gary is paid through a set fee (currently $250) for his specialized consulting service.

Benny sells a direct product (language hacking guide) for a fixed price from his website.

Megan also sells a direct product (custom dresses and wedding accessories), but her pricing is variable.

Mignon provides her popular podcast service for free to listeners, underwritten by advertising and sponsorship.

Each model has specific strengths and disadvantages. Gary makes $250 at a time . . . but then has to "earn" the fee by arranging someone's travel. Benny sells his guide for just $29 . . . but the process is automated and he doesn't have to do anything after the money comes in.

Megan sells a variety of products (and also owns the co-working space), so her income is diversified . . . but the main project of making wedding dresses is labor-intensive. Mignon's sponsors provide reliable, regular income . . . but she loses a certain amount of control by introducing advertising in her communication to the audience.

Despite the differences, the core goal for each of these approaches is finding the right kind of product or service for the right group of people. Without the right fit, none of the projects would be successful. But when you find the formula, there's no denying that a business built on the right kind of passion can be highly successful.

In Venice, California, Gabriella Redding built a million-dollar hula-hoop business after losing weight through hooping. Before that she was a tattoo artist and then a restaurant owner. "I'm an artist," she told *Forbes* magazine. "Artists are serial entrepreneurs because we have to figure out ways to sell our work. It's either that or you become a starving artist, and I'm not a starving artist."

Compared with working just to make a living, it's much easier to do what you love and get paid for it. You just have to find the right passion, the right audience, and the right business model.

KEY POINTS

· As in the examples of Gary and Benny, good businesses provide solutions to problems: "What do I do with all these extra frequent flyer miles?" "How can I easily learn a new language?"

· Many follow-your-passion businesses are built on something indirectly related, not the passion or hobby itself. When considering an opportunity, ask: "Where is the business model?"

· Not every passion or hobby is worth building into a business, and not everyone will want to have a business that is based on a passion or hobby.

· You can establish a specialized consulting business in one day—the more specific, the better.

4 • The Rise of the Roaming Entrepreneur

"LOCATION, LOCATION, LOCATION"
IS OVERRATED.

"A desk is a dangerous place from which to view the world."

—JOHN LE CARRÉ

Packing a carry-on bag with running shoes and two changes of clothes, I head out into the world via a short connection from Portland to Vancouver International Airport. Later that evening, the twelve-hour Cathay Pacific flight to Hong Kong gives me two hours to watch a movie, six hours to sleep, and four hours to write emails.

Arriving in Asia, I clear immigration (no bags to claim), check my wallet to see if I still have local currency from the last trip here, and settle into a concourse chair before jumping on the train into the city. I flip open the laptop, connect to "HKG-Free-WiFi," and log onto the world. *Whoosh* . . . out go all the emails I wrote on the plane, and in come 150 more that arrived during the night.

I check in with Reese, my designer, about a project we've been working on. I answer customer support requests—a page on our site is down, someone needs a login, and so on—and write a quick update to customers. I review reader comments from my latest blog post and quickly check my daily list of email signups, the only metric I monitor on a frequent basis. (If all's going well with new subscribers, everything else should be OK.)

I often stay in guest houses and hostels, but later tonight I have a conference call scheduled for the bleary hour of 2 a.m.—it's daytime in North America—so I head to the Conrad Hotel. Fortunately, I slept enough on the plane that I'm good to go after a shower, so I set up shop in my "office" for the next two days. A few hours later, the host on the call is saying "good afternoon" to everyone, and I try to refrain from mentioning the local time while looking out at the Hong Kong skyline.

On this trip I'm headed on to Vietnam and Laos, but I could be going anywhere. After I adjust to the time difference over the next couple of days, I settle into a routine of morning work and afternoon exploration. At least one week a month, I live in this dream world of travel, work, and frequent coffee breaks. The business is structured around my life, not the other way around.

I know what some people think: It sounds like a fantasy. Well . . . it really is happening, on a broad scale, for thousands of people all over the world. My example is just one of many; let's hear about a few others.

Case Study 1: The Music Teacher

In 2009, Brandon Pearce was living in Utah and working as a successful piano teacher, meaning that he got by and paid the rent while doing something he enjoyed. But Brandon was also intensely curious, and wanted to combine an interest in technology with his passion for music education. As he thought about colleagues he knew, he found the convergence point between his skill and what they needed.

"Music teachers don't want to deal with business administration; they want to teach music," he said. "But in the typical music teacher's workday, they have to spend much of their time dealing with administrative tasks." Scheduling, rescheduling, sending reminders—in addition to time, all these things take up a lot of attention and distract from teaching. Furthermore, many music teachers aren't making all the money they should, since payments are sometimes overlooked and students fail to show up.

Brandon didn't intend to create a business at first; he just wanted to solve what he called the "disorganized music teacher problem" for himself. The answer was Music Teacher's Helper, an interface that Brandon created for personal use before turning it into a one-stop platform for music teachers of all kinds. The teachers could create their own websites (without having any technical skills) and handle all aspects of scheduling and billing, thus enabling them to focus on the actual teaching they enjoyed.

Was this a market in search of a solution? Yes, and the market was substantial. Was Brandon giving them the fish? Yes, and because music teachers are often on a low budget, Brandon made sure to highlight the fact that paying for Music Teacher's Helper might actually *save* them money over time, but to ensure the business's profitability, he didn't skimp on the price. The service is available in several different versions, including a free version for limited use and going up to a $588-a-year version depending on the number of students.*

Three years later, Brandon's life is quite different. Instead of living in Utah, he now wakes up in sunny Escazú, Costa Rica, where he lives with his wife and three young daughters. He has

---

*The specific pricing model that Brandon chose for his business is an important factor in its profitability. We'll look at pricing and how it relates to overall income in Chapters 10 and 11.

ten employees living in different places around the world. He carefully tracks his time and estimates that he spends eight to fifteen hours a week directly related to the business. The rest of his time is spent with his family and on various side projects that he pursues for fun.

Brandon and his family used to live in Utah and now they live in Costa Rica, but that's not the whole story; the whole story is that they could live anywhere they want. When they needed to do a visa run, they went over to Guatemala for eight days, and since Brandon and his wife are "unschooling" their children and can easily take them anywhere, there's no telling where they'll end up next. (A tentative plan involves moving to Asia.)

Oh, and one more thing: Music Teacher's Helper is currently on track to earn at least $360,000 a year. Because his customers commit for the long term and pay monthly, it's unlikely that this number will ever go down. Instead, it will continue to increase as more and more music teachers join the ranks.

Case Study 2:
The Accidental Worldwide Photographer

Originally from Michigan, Kyle Hepp is an "accidental" entrepreneur in the literal sense. Having relocated to Chile with her husband, Seba, Kyle made ends meet by working on side projects for AOL while she looked for a job in her planned field of sports management. The South American lifestyle was great, but Seba's job as a construction engineer was far from secure, and the company started to go under. One Friday afternoon, he received notice that his salary was being cut 20 percent. He declined to sign a new contract and was immediately let go.

Two days after learning of the layoff, Kyle was out jogging when tragedy struck in the form of a pickup truck that ran into her at a crowded intersection, sending her flying a hundred feet from the point of impact. Her injuries weren't life-threatening or permanent, but as you'd expect, Kyle was badly hurt. After a week in the hospital, she spent several more weeks at home, unable to walk and with so many bruises that she couldn't even type—thus ending the side gig with AOL, which was done on a contract basis. "Between my husband's layoff and getting run over by the car," Kyle told me with a straight face, "it was kind of a bad weekend."

Kyle and Seba had been married for nearly three years at that point and hadn't ever had a real honeymoon, so they decided they might as well take vacation time while they could. Instead of looking for work, they booked flights to Italy and spent several weeks seeing Europe for the first time. Before the accident, Kyle had been dabbling in wedding photography. She had never really tried to make a career of it, but before flying out she updated her website and announced that she was accepting new bookings. A request came in right away, giving Kyle confidence that she might be able to make some kind of career out of it.

When they returned to Chile, Kyle and Seba decided to try photography full-time, "at least until the bookings stopped coming and the money ran out." To their surprise, request after request arrived in Kyle's inbox, and the schedule quickly filled up. Two years later, they were making $90,000 a year and were fully booked another year in advance.

They now work all over the world, doing weddings in Argentina, Spain, England, and the United States. You might wonder what the big deal is with Kyle's work—since there is no shortage of other good photographers available locally, why do clients fly her from country to country? Kyle says that her clients are usually well traveled themselves, and aren't afraid of hiring someone from afar. "They know that the world is a small place," she says, "and they like our work because we build relationships over time."

Case Study 3: The Spreadsheet King*

A description of Bernard Vukas's work space is typical of roaming entrepreneurs: "I work from anywhere, anytime. Time zone and location are irrelevant. All my property fits in a single backpack, including the laptop," he told me in an email from a beach in Koh Tao, Thailand, where he was living on an indefinite basis. Bernard is from Croatia, which has nice beaches of its own, but he wanted to see more of the world.

Bernard helps companies that use Microsoft Office applications to process large amounts of data, creating or modifying extensions that make the data easier to manage. Bernard started by pricing at a decent wage by Croatian standards but much lower than what North American companies were used to paying. This strategy worked well in helping him establish a client base and a good reputation, but the best business decision came when he tripled his rates for new clients.

One day, Bernard made $720 on a big project. Reflecting on the amount's significance, he wrote: "Many people on a minimum salary in Croatia are getting this amount in one month. People who get double that amount are considered well paid. To have it all come in on a single day is unheard of." Bernard might return to his country of origin at some point, but it was hard to imagine him ever returning to another way of life.

---

*Bernard, the "Spreadsheet King," is a different guy from Purna, "Mr. Spreadsheet." Lesson: At least in the world of spreadsheets, there's always room for one more.

A Brief Primer for Location Independence

- It's usually easier to operate a business while roaming the world than it is to start one. Be sure to spend plenty of time getting set up before you hit the road.

- With a U.S. or Canadian passport, you can stay for up to ninety days in many different countries around the world. In some of them, you can do a "visa run" across the border after the time is up and then return for another extended stay.

- You can learn about the visas required for different countries by visiting VisaHQ.com or VisaHQ.ca, a commercial service I use for my own visa applications. Other companies offer the same assistance, and you don't need to use a service to apply for visas if you're not traveling that frequently.

- As much as possible, keep your work "in the cloud" by using online services such as Google Docs and Dropbox. This way, you can access it from anywhere and don't have to worry as much about keeping your data with you.

- Change your password frequently, and don't use the name of your cat as the password (not that I learned this through experience or anything . . .).

- Stay for free with helpful hosts through CouchSurfing.org, or at low cost from individual landlords at AirBnB.com.

- You can start from anywhere, but as a general recommendation, Latin America and Southeast Asia are two of the easiest and most hospitable regions to begin your nomadic adventures.

- Some places are more tech-friendly than others. To be aware of what to expect before visiting a new country, study up by reading the forums at BootsnAll.com or MeetPlanGo.com.

- As you roam, maintain a balance between adventure and work. Remember that most people work regular jobs and travel only once

> in a while, so be sure to take advantage of sightseeing and experiencing the local culture. But similarly, don't feel bad about needing to devote more hours to work whenever needed. It's OK; the work allows you to travel.

Digital nomads and roaming entrepreneurs come in all packages, and it's hard to get away from their infectious stories. As I interviewed business owners and put the word out for more submissions, I kept hearing story after story that sounded like those of Brandon, Kyle, and Bernard. I'd continue to cast the net for more traditional businesses, but I kept thinking: *This is a great business model.* Why would you want to do anything else?

In these examples, Brandon is a music teacher, Kyle is a photographer, and Bernard is a developer. The list could go on: Cherie Ve Ard, whom we'll meet in Chapter 13, is a health-care consultant, and Brandy Agerbeck, whose story is in Chapter 7, is a graphic facilitator. Because of the nature of their work, many of the businesses in the other case studies are technically location independent even if they currently have a fixed address. There is more than one road to the road, in other words, but one business model is especially useful for location independence: the business of information publishing. Since this model is both common and highly profitable, let's look at it in some detail.

Become Your Own Publisher

As the founder of 800-CEO-READ, a leading retailer of business books, Jack Covert is a veteran of both traditional publishing and self-publishing. I asked Jack what has changed about the publishing world in recent years. "Everything's changed," he said. "We've always seen authors self-publish their works, but never to such a wide extent. What's different is the quality of the work. These days, a number of self-published works have at least as good a quality as do books from big publishers. The playing field has been greatly leveled, and continues to be."

The other thing that's different, Jack told me, is that most authors chose self-publishing in the past because they couldn't get a traditional publisher to purchase their work. Today, some authors are deliberately choosing to distribute their work directly, even turning down significant offers in favor of going it alone.*

But hey, who needs books? You don't need to be an author or even think of yourself as a writer to take advantage of this changing world. Digital publishing tends to fit into at least a few categories: one-off products, fixed-period courses, and recurring subscriptions.

Jen Lemen and Andrea Scher, two friends who had attended a retreat together, had an idea to start an online course for women. They called it Mondo Beyondo, and created a community model for participants to post their life lists, goals, and ideas. On the other side of the Atlantic, former journalist Susannah Conway was independently setting up a similar project called Unravelling. Thousands of participants later, both projects have long waiting lists for future sessions, and both produce six-figure annual incomes. Part of the beauty of this model is that it grows predominantly by referral. As students finish the four- or five-week courses, many of them tell their friends, who then sign up for the next session.

A few people have created true scale in their online publishing efforts. In Melbourne, Australia, Darren Rowse created a popular photography forum that attracted more than 300,000 subscribers

---

*One frequently cited example is Barry Eisler, who turned down a $500,000 offer for one of his books. However, he has a sizable following and an established track record that new authors lack.

in less than three years. He also founded ProBlogger, a hub for new digital publishers seeking to learn the ropes. In Texas, Brian Clark runs a company that provides online services, including website themes and marketing advice. Many customers arrive from Brian's writing on CopyBlogger.com and related sites. The business employs a dozen people and earns more than $5 million a year, in large part thanks to reliance on recurring subscriptions. (We'll discuss subscriptions and hear more from Brian in Chapter 10.)

A cynic might wonder, Is there really so much market space for all of these projects? Long story short, the answer is yes. These examples aren't highly unusual, and I had to decline many additional stories because this book is not strictly about information publishing. Some parts of information publishing are still in a Wild West stage, but this strong business model is here to stay.

Like everything else under the sun, this "new" business isn't entirely new. As Jack from 800-CEO-READ mentioned, some independent publishers have always known that it's often better to sell direct. What's changed is the speed, quality, and potential to reach a much broader audience. That's what these roaming publishers are doing—and a guy in Fullerton, California, provides a typical example.

The $120,000 E-Book

Brett Kelly, a self-described "professional geek" who worked as a software developer, had a busy job and a stressful home life. As a result of $15,000 of credit card debt and the high cost of Southern California living, Brett and his wife, Joana, worked opposite schedules to make ends meet. "I'd get home and trade off with a high-five to Joana as she went to work at a restaurant," he told me as we sat at a taco stand in Los Angeles. "The last few months, we were both tired all the time, the kids were unhappy, and the overall situation wasn't good."

For years, Brett had watched from the sidelines as friends and colleagues started profitable projects and either quit their jobs or established an additional income stream. Finally, he had an idea of his own: As a power user of Evernote, the free note-keeping software, Brett noticed that there was no detailed user manual for people to get the most out of the service.*

Brett spent months carefully documenting every tip and trick he could find about Evernote, compiling everything with detailed screenshots and tutorials into a big PDF file. "I obsessed over this thing," he said, "and I wanted to make sure I got everything exactly right." When he sent me a draft of what would become *Evernote Essentials,* I was impressed. Many e-book writers pad their products with superfluous copy, big fonts, and wide margins. Brett's was the opposite: The finished product weighed in at more than ninety pages of solid content. Nevertheless, solid content isn't everything; you also have to sell something that people are willing to spend money on. Would they?

Right before the guide went on sale, Brett made a deal with Joana: If he sold at least $10,000 worth of copies, she would quit her job waiting tables at the restaurant and stay at home with their two kids full-time. Brett estimated that it would take months, if not longer, to reach the $10k goal . . . but just eleven days after *Evernote Essentials* went on sale, the PayPal account tipped into five figures. (Being the geek that he was, Brett promptly took a screenshot on his iPhone and made it his wallpaper.) Less than twenty-four hours later, Joana put in her two-week notice at the restaurant. Aside from brief breaks when the kids were born, this would be the first time she didn't work in their seven years of parenthood.

---

*Technically, there was no English-language manual; more than a dozen books or guides on Evernote already existed in Japan. This suggested the strong marketability of the project *and* revealed a gap in the English-language marketplace that Brett was able to fill.

Months later, sales of *Evernote Essentials* continued to bring in at least $300 a day, projecting annual revenue of more than $120,000 for something that was essentially a side project. Interestingly, if the project had been produced as a print book from a traditional publisher, those numbers could be considered a failure—author royalties would have brought Brett only around $18 a day. But since Brett was the sole owner and delivery was digital, the $300 that arrived in his PayPal account every day was almost entirely profit.

In an odd twist, the executives who developed Evernote got word of the guide and sent Brett a note that they wanted to talk. Brett was worried they were upset about him making money from their free product, but the opposite was true: The CEO loved it and wanted to hire him. Brett left the boring full-time job and took on a new role at Evernote, with the understanding that he could continue to sell the guide and retain all profits while working at home for the company. Sweet! Here's how Brett describes the end results:

> The unreal success of this project has not only freed our family from a decade of debt and financial instability but has also given us the freedom to pursue the kind of life we want. Since I now work from home and Joana is a stay-at-home mom, we spend far more time with our kids than most people could hope for. There are times when I still can't believe it's actually happened, and I couldn't be more thankful.

Brett's project had all the predictors of success we've considered thus far: It began with something he was both passionate about and skilled in, and then he forged his knowledge into a useful package that could be acquired instantly by users. If you wanted to learn about Evernote but didn't want to spend the time surfing around, a $25 investment could solve the problem. The choice of price was also perfect: Brett could have priced much lower, as some digital publishers do, but he chose to take a stand and provide a clear value proposition to his potential customers.

Become Your Own Publisher

Follow these steps to enter the information publishing business. Each step can be made more complicated, but they all relate to this basic outline.

1. Find a topic that people will pay to learn about. It helps if you are an expert in the topic, but if not, that's what research is for.

2. Capture the information in one of three ways:

   a. Write it down.

   b. Record audio or video.

   c. Produce some combination of a and b.

3. Combine your materials into a *product:* an e-book or digital package that can be downloaded by buyers.

4. Create an offer. What exactly are you selling, and why should people take action on it? Learn more about offers in Chapter 7.

5. Decide on a fair, value-based price for your offer. For pricing guidelines, see Chapters 10 and 11.

6. Find a way to get paid. PayPal.com is the most ubiquitous method, with the ability to accept payment from users in more than 180 countries. Other options are available if you want more flexibility.*

7. Publish the offer and get the word out. For an overview of hustling, see Chapter 9.

8. Cash in and head to the beach! (This step may require further effort.)

*You can find a review of several different payment options in the online resources at 100startup.com.

Alas, like any trend or business model, not every story of independent publishing is a success. Many aspiring publishers operate on an "if you build it, they will come" model. Later in the book, we'll rename it the "if you build it, they *might* come" model—sometimes it works, but many times it doesn't, and there's no guarantee of instant riches. For every online course that becomes a Mondo Beyondo-size success, many others flounder on with five participants. For every $120,000 e-book like Brett's, many others sell two copies (one to the writer's grandmother and one to a friend of the family) before fizzling out.

Some of the failures relate to unrealistic expectations. Put simply, some people want the sun and the fun (or the $300 a day) without the work. Partly as a result of the allure of working from anywhere, many aspiring entrepreneurs focus much more on the "anywhere" part than they do the "work" part. Since the work part is what sustains everything else, it's better to focus on it from the beginning. After all, the best thing about a location-independent business is *possibility*. The fact that you can head off to Argentina or Thailand on a whim doesn't necessarily mean that you actually will.

The classic image of a roaming entrepreneur usually involves a guy or girl sitting on the beach in a swimsuit, drink nearby, with a laptop propped up against the backdrop of a sunset. My limited attempts at replicating such a scene usually involve worrying about the laptop (Will it get stolen? Will I get sand in the keyboard?) and straining to see the screen against the glare of the sun. Furthermore, most beaches in tropical locales do not provide WiFi access, and for that matter, plenty of other places don't either—so if you're going to operate your business on the road, you'll need to learn to think about your business as much as you think about being on the road.

It's just like following your passion to the bank: Some people prefer to keep their passion on the side, and some people prefer not to mix their vacations with their work. Even entrepreneurs like Brandon Pearce who have carefully built a high-income, hands-free business that allows them to work minimal hours do that only *after* the business has been established. In the beginning, there's usually a fair amount of fumbling and a large number of hours spent working on projects that may or may not succeed.

But hey, that's enough of a reality check. There's no doubt that thousands of people have established successful businesses on this model, especially over the last decade. Why not follow in their path, charting your own course along the way?

When I last talked with Brandon, he was still doing extremely well (up to $30,000 a month in our most recent conversation). He was now branching out into new areas in Costa Rica and beyond, even thinking about buying shares in a local farm. Perhaps the farm won't be as profitable as the online project, but that's OK—month after month, the income from the music software will continue to roll in. Brandon and his family have established complete freedom and the ability to make a new life wherever it leads them. Every day is an adventure.

KEY POINTS

- Roaming entrepreneurs are everywhere these days. Many of them are quietly building significant (six figures or higher) businesses while living in paradise.

- Just as not every passion leads to a good business model, a lot of people pursue the nomadic lifestyle for the wrong reasons. The best question to answer is: What do *you* want to do?

- There are many roads to location independence, but the business of information publishing is especially profitable. (And there's more than one path to information publishing; it isn't just about e-books.)

· Everything relates to the lessons that began in Chapter 1: Find the convergence between what you love and what other people are willing to buy, remember that you're probably good at more than one thing, and combine passion and usefulness to build a real business—no matter where you end up living.

5 • The New Demographics

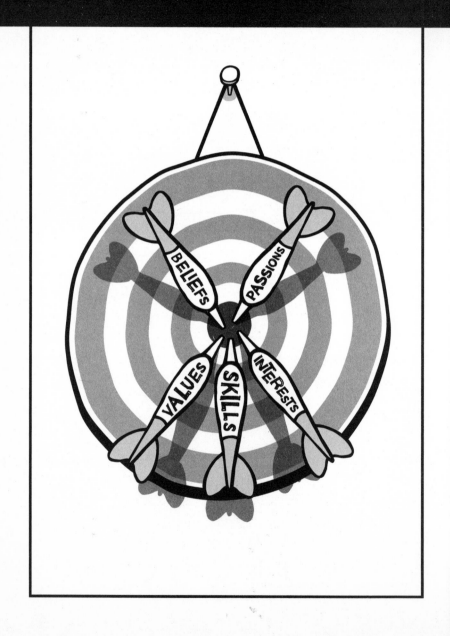

**"Business opportunities are like buses;
there's always another one coming."**

—RICHARD BRANSON

The frequent references to customers and clients lead to a good question: Who are they? And just as important, *where* are they and how do you find them? As you consider these questions, it may help to fit your ideal customers into traditional demographics—things such as age, gender, income—or it may not.

While I was writing my first book, different people in the publishing industry asked me about the "target market" for the community that was rapidly growing. I'd been in business for a while, so I knew what they meant, but I couldn't figure out how to explain the diverse group of people who read my blog. We had artists, travelers, high school students trying to decide whether to go to college or strike out on their own, retired people making plans for a new chapter in their lives, and everyone in between. There were a number of entrepreneurs and self-employed folks but also a lot of people in traditional jobs. The gender ratio was split almost evenly between men and women.

Finally, I realized that the target market had nothing to do with demographics in a traditional sense—the group simply consisted of people from all backgrounds who wanted to live unconventional, remarkable lives. They were "pro-change" and interested in pursuing a big dream while also making the world a better place for others. In other words, I didn't have to segment or label them according to irrelevant categories.

You may not want to be a writer, but as you explore different possibilities on the road to freedom and value, it helps to think clearly about the people you plan to serve. There are now at least two ways to group them together.

Traditional Demographics:	*New Demographics:*
Age, Location, Sex/Gender, Race/Ethnicity, Income	Interests, Passions, Skills, Beliefs, Values*

In Arcata, California, the husband and wife team of Mark Ritz and Charlie Jordan own the Kinetic Koffee Company. KKC is a gourmet "microroaster" that makes great coffee . . . but these days there is no shortage of great coffee, so they needed something more. KKC found its legs and became profitable by targeting a specific group: cyclists, skiers, backpackers, and "pretty much anyone who enjoys the outdoor lifestyle." By focusing on enthusiasts, they immediately set KKC apart in a crowded market.

Mark and Charlie's connection to the outdoors is natural. Before starting the business, Mark had spent most of his career working in the cycling industry. Charlie was vice president of a kayak company, and both of them were active in the local racing and recreational communities. They were also coffee addicts, so combining the two passions seemed like the right approach. "We weren't the first coffee company to target the cycling market," Mark told me, "but we

---

*This sometimes is known as *psychographics*.

were the first to look at the market from the perspective of the bicycle shops and outdoor dealers. We have now outlived a number of better-financed companies who have since left the market."

Outdoor enthusiasts are KKC's people, but to reach them, Mark and Charlie work with bicycle shops and outdoor stores. Maintaining good relationships with the distributors ensures access to almost every store in the country, and Mark complements this strategy by visiting trade shows and consumer events. Donating 10 percent of profits to outdoor causes every year, KKC is a low-six-figure business.

The Internet has made it much easier to connect with people through shared values and ideals, but it's not strictly an online phenomenon. More than thirty years ago, long before Facebook, a band with an underground following figured this out. Here's what Jerry Garcia said about the Grateful Dead's followers:

> There's a lot of that stuff with people bringing their kids, kids bringing their parents, people bringing their grandparents—it's gotten to be really stretched out now. It was never my intention to say, this is the demographics of our audience. It just happened.

Tom Bihn, a bag manufacturer from Seattle, Washington, gives us a similar idea: "We're consistently and pleasantly surprised by the diversity of our customers. People have a natural desire to categorize and quantify, but we've always felt doing so with our customers would be pointless. They're students, artists, businesspeople, teachers, scientists, programmers, photographers, parents, designers, farmers, and philanthropists." (Read more of Tom's story in Chapter 13.)

Changing the "Who"

A busy working mother from Hudson, Ohio, Kris Murray saw an opportunity in helping child care providers run their businesses more effectively. For years she dutifully worked at building relationships one by one with day-care centers, only to get frustrated with their low prices and lack of interest in developing the business.

Despite the challenges, Kris knew it could be a good business. Families will always need child care, and child care providers are usually more focused on providing quality service than on managing the business side of things. How could Kris break through with a successful offer, and how could she boost her income as she served her clients? The early days were discouraging. She was exhausted, overwhelmed, and ready to quit.

Then something changed. First, she streamlined her services, making them more oriented to what her clients clearly wanted—she learned to give them the fish. But the second change was also important. In Kris's words, she found a way to "change the WHO": the clients she worked with. Many day-care centers were microbusinesses themselves, run by one or two people. Although these centers may provide good child care, they tend to be wary of investing in services and therefore aren't the best fit for Kris's consulting practice.

Pivoting to a more desirable market, Kris created a new division of products and services targeted to multilocation center owners. These owners had a much larger investment in their businesses and could afford to pay more for marketing help. The change made a huge difference on the bottom line. Kris went from "doing OK" to making more than $20,000 a month. In the early days, she tried to sell something that her clients weren't ready for. She fixed the problem by changing two things: what she offered and to whom she offered it.

Disaster and Recovery:
CULTURE SHOCK EDITION

Ridlon Kiphart, AKA Sharkman, has one of those jobs everyone envies—he's a self-titled CAO, or chief adventure officer, of a small company called Live Adventurously. After previous career stints as a trapeze artist, divemaster, charity founder, and "watersports dude" on a cruise ship, he now runs his own show, hosting trips to exotic locations. I asked Sharkman about his greatest challenge in the new business, and here's how he tells the story of a misadventure in the South Pacific.

The best and worst days were the same day. We had finished the first half of the first trip in Fiji, and the guests were raving. We returned from a day spent diving turquoise waters to find a long white linen-draped dinner table sitting on the sand at water's edge. It was surrounded by tiki torches and set beautifully. With the sun setting and island music playing in the warm air, we gathered with our friends for one of the most spectacular dinners in history . . . right up until the phone call came in.

The experience was like listening to a beautiful song and then abruptly hearing the needle from the record player rip across the album. The news was that the paramount chief from the neighboring island we had planned to visit the next day had died, and the mourning ritual required that everything be shut down for the next 100 (!) nights. We had nine exultant guests and nowhere to go.

This was when doing our research earlier and really knowing the area paid off. We managed to extend our stay where we were by one night and spent the time feverishly cobbling together plans. We chartered an aircraft (dubbed the flying coffin for self-explanatory reasons); contacted numerous hotels, resorts, and dive operators; got recommendations; did some more research; and booked the group into a newly opened property on a remote island. The transition went smoothly, the entire rest of the trip came off without a hitch, and it was as if it had been planned that way the entire time.

In the end, the resort we were originally booked into kept half our money despite being in breach of contract. Their attitude was if you want us, you'll have to come and get us. That showed us how worthless contracts can be overseas. Our guests rallied to us and offered to pay the additional money, but we declined and ate the loss. It wasn't our guests' fault, and they shouldn't have to pay. It was a hell of a way to start a new business—taking a big financial hit—but it was the right thing to do. That's the way we've chosen to operate, and I believe it always pays off.

How can you follow in the footsteps of Tom Bihn, the Kinetic Koffee Company, Kris Murray, and even the Grateful Dead?

Strategy 1: Latch on to a Popular Hobby, Passion, or Craze

Popular diet plans come and go, but a few of them stick around. The Paleo diet, which encourages its followers to eat a lot of some things (meat and uncooked vegetables) and very little or none of other things (grains, dairy, sugars, etc.) looks like it's here to stay. Like all strict diets, Paleo attracts a passionate following in addition to a passionate group on the other side that questions its scientific basis. Situations like these—an industry or movement with lots of lovers and haters—always present a good business opportunity.

Enter Jason Glaspey, who had adopted the lifestyle after reading *The Paleo Diet*, a popular manual for Paleo followers. Jason noticed a big difficulty with trying to follow the diet: It was complicated. "Eat natural food and avoid grains" sounds simple enough, but adhering to the whole diet requires a fair amount of ongoing planning. This is another sign of a good business opportunity: when lots of people are interested in something but have a hard time implementing it in their daily lives.

Jason got to work creating a solution. He understood that the demographics for hardcore Paleo followers were more male than female and tended to fall in the age range of twenty-five to thirty-five. More important, however, Jason noticed that people of various backgrounds were attracted to the Paleo lifestyle but weren't sure they could devote much of their time to planning for it. Thus the opportunity: Provide a comprehensive resource that "gave them the fish" (no pun intended, although Paleo followers do eat a lot of fish) by telling them exactly what to buy, cook, and eat each week. Jason started Paleo Plan, a one-man business, in three weeks with $1,500. Within a year, the business grew to earn recurring income of more than $6,000 a month, requiring a grand total of two hours' work to update the site each week.

Strategy 2: Sell What People Buy (and Ask Them If You're Not Sure)

As you focus on getting to know "your people," keep this important principle in mind: Most of us like to buy, but we don't like to be sold. Old-school marketing is based on *persuasion*; new marketing is based on *invitation*. With persuasion marketing, you're trying to convince people of something, whether it's the need for your service in general or why your particular offering is better than the competition's. A persuasion marketer is like a door-to-door vacuum cleaner salesman: If he knocks on enough doors, he might eventually sell a vacuum cleaner . . . but at great personal cost and much rejection.

Persuasion marketing is still around and always will be, but now there's an alternative. If you don't want to go door to door with a vacuum cleaner in hand, consider how the people in our study have created businesses that customers desperately want to be a part of.

What do you sell? Remember the lesson from Chapter 2: Find out what people want and find a way to give it to them. As you build a tribe of committed fans and loyal customers, they'll eagerly await your new offers, ready to pounce as soon as they go live. This way isn't just new; it's also better.

When you're brainstorming different ideas and aren't sure which one is best, one of the most effective ways to figure it out is simply to ask your prospects, your current customers (if you have them), or anyone you think might be a good fit for your idea. It helps to be specific; asking people if they "like" something isn't very helpful. Since you're trying to build a business, not just a hobby, a better method is to ask if they'd be willing to pay for what you're selling. This separates merely "liking" something from actually paying for it.

Questions like these are good starting points:

- What is your biggest problem with _____?
- What is the number one question you have about _____?
- What can I do to help you with _____?

Fill in the blanks with the specific topic, niche, or industry you're researching: "What is your biggest problem with getting things done?" or "What is the number one question you have about online dating?"

The fun thing about this kind of research, especially the open-ended questions to which people can respond however they'd like, is that you'll often learn things you had no idea about before. It's also a way to build momentum toward a big launch or relaunch, something we'll look at more in Chapter 8.

You can ask for input either on a small, one-on-one basis or on a group basis. To check with a broader group of respondents, I use a paid service provided by SurveyMonkey.com, but you can also create a free, less sophisticated version with Google Forms (available within Google Docs). Write to your group of respondents, tell them what you're thinking about, and ask for help. It's good to keep the survey very simple: Ask only what you need to know. All of us are busy, but if you construct a good survey, the response rate can be 50 percent or higher.

Once you've moved beyond the basics and have a good idea of what you're hoping to offer, you can take this process further. I often write to my customer list and ask about specific product ideas, like this:

> Here are a few projects I'm thinking about working on during the next few months, but I could be totally wrong. Please let me know what you think of each idea.
>
> Idea 1
> Idea 2
> Idea 3
> etc.

I then apply a simple ranking scale to each idea and ask the respondents to stick with their first impression. The ranking scale usually consists of answers such as "I love it!" "You should do it," "Sounds interesting," "Would need to hear more," and "It's not for me."

Generally speaking, it's good to keep surveys to less than ten questions or so. To get more overall responses, ask fewer questions. To get more detailed responses (but from fewer people), ask more questions. It's up to you, but make sure that whatever you ask is something you actually need to know about. Pay close attention to the feedback; it will either confirm your intention to proceed or make you think about restructuring your proposed project.

Either way, the information is valuable, but also remember that the majority opinion isn't everything. Among other concerns, you'll need your own motivations for building a project over time. If your motivations are based strictly on the preferences of someone else, you'll run the risks of boredom, unhappiness, and simply being less purposeful than you could be otherwise. The lesson is to use surveys but use them carefully. Sometimes, deciding not to pursue a promising project or deliberately turning away business is one of the most powerful things you can do. (See "The Customer Is Often Wrong" for a story about that.)

The Customer Is ~~Always Right~~ Often Wrong

It was a big launch day, which meant I was up by 5 a.m., coffee in hand and ready to go. As the new website went live, hundreds of customers were ready and waiting to purchase. I watched the shopping cart fill up and closely monitored the in-box for support issues.

Happily, the launch was successful. By noon, more than a thousand people had purchased, and that number would double by the end of the day. I had sent so many customer thank-you emails that Google briefly shut down my email account, thinking I was a spammer. A friend at the company rescued me by restoring the account, and I went back to plowing through messages. In the in-box were hundreds of notes from excited new customers, as well as dozens of minor support requests: "I lost my password," "The site is down," "How can I change my log-in?" and so on.

And then there was Dan. The note from Dan read, "I'd like a refund." I wrote him back quickly, "No problem, but what's wrong?"

"Let me give you some free advice," Dan wrote in a tone that was obviously sarcastic. "Give me a call and I'll tell you how you lost my business."

I looked at the shopping cart and the site comments—several orders and dozens of excited messages were coming through every minute—and replied to Dan: "Sorry, I can't call you. I'll issue the refund and I wish you well, but I don't need any advice right now."

You've probably heard the expression "The customer is always right," but most small business owners quickly discover this is not true. Yes, you want to focus on meeting people's needs and going above and beyond them whenever you can, but any single customer does not always know what's best for your whole business. These customers may not be the right ones for your business, and there's nothing wrong with saying farewell to them so you can focus on serving other people.

I didn't have time to call Dan on launch day, and perhaps I missed a good opportunity to learn from him. But I'm pretty sure it was the better decision to get back to work on my core market instead of spending time with one disgruntled customer who had already received a refund.

The Possibilities List and the Decision-Making Matrix

As you learn more about your customers and what they want, you may find yourself overwhelmed with ideas. What should you do when you have more ideas than time to pursue them? Two things: First, make sure you're capturing all the ideas and writing them down, since you might want them later; second, find a way to evaluate competing ideas. Creating a "possibilities list" helps you retain ideas for when you have more time to implement them.

Most of the time, however, *having* an idea isn't a problem for entrepreneurs.* Once you begin to think of opportunities, you'll probably end up with no shortage of ideas written on napkins, scrawled in notebooks, and floating around in your head. The

*See "Where Do Ideas Come From?" on page 27.

problem is evaluating which projects are worth pursuing, and then deciding between different ideas. Sometimes you may know intuitively what the best move is. In those cases, you should proceed without hesitation. Other times, though, you'll feel conflicted. What should you do?

The decision-making matrix will help you evaluate a range of projects and separate the winners from the "maybe laters." Putting something off doesn't mean you'll never do it, but prioritization will help you get started on what makes the most impact. First of all, keep in mind the most basic questions of any successful microbusiness:

- Does the project produce an obvious product or service?
- Do you know people who will want to buy it? (Or do you know where to find them?)
- Do you have a way to get paid?

Those questions form a simple baseline evaluation. If you don't have a clear yes on one of them, go back to the drawing board. Let's assume, however, that you can answer yes to all of them but know you can't pursue five big projects at one time. In that case, you'll need some method of evaluation. Here's one option: the decision-making matrix.

	Impact	Effort	Profitability	Vision	Sum
Idea 1					
Idea 2					
Idea 3					
Idea 4					
Idea 5					

In this matrix, you'll list your ideas in the left-hand column and then score them on a scale of 1 to 5, with 5 being the highest. Granted, the scoring will be subjective, but since we're looking for trends, it's OK to estimate. Score your ideas according to these criteria:

Impact: Overall, how much of an impact will this project make on your business and customers?

Effort: How much time and work will it take to create the project? (In this case, a lower score indicates more effort, so choose 1 for a project that requires a ton of work and 5 for a project that requires almost no work.)

Profitability: Relative to the other ideas, how much money will the project bring in?

Vision: How close of a fit is this project with your overall mission and vision?

Rank each item on a scale of 1 to 5 and then add them up in the right-hand column. Remember, you're looking for trends. If you have to cut one project, cut the lowest one; if you can only take on one project, proceed with the highest one.

Here's an example from my own business, when I was deciding which business projects to pursue in the second half of 2011:

	Impact	Effort	Profitability	Fit with Vision	Total
Publishing Guide	4	3	3	5	15
Empire Building Kit	4	2	5	4	15
Community-Building Webinar	3	4	2	3	12
Shopping Cart Project	3	3	3	3	12
Small Live Workshops	4	1	1	4	10

When you don't know where to start and have a bunch of ideas, this exercise can help. In my case, the live workshops would have a big impact on the people who attended them (or so I hoped) but not on anyone else. They would require a great deal of prep time and energy and wouldn't be very profitable. Therefore, I put them on hold.

The decision-making matrix also helps you see the strengths and weaknesses of your ideas. I liked the idea of small live workshops until I realized they would require a great deal of work for little reward and impact. That was a big weakness! On the other hand, a project like the webinar represented a middle ground: I didn't expect the workload to be overwhelming, and I expected it to deliver above-average (although not amazing) results.

• • •

When we last left off with James Kirk in Chapter 1, he had moved from Seattle to South Carolina and opened the coffee shop he had been thinking about for the last six months. What happened next? As he settled into a slower way of life and got to know his customers, he made a few changes. "I learned there was no way you could have a breakfast place down here and not sell biscuits," he said. "If you had told me back in Seattle that my coffee shop would sell biscuits, I would have laughed." He also sold a great deal of iced tea almost every day of the year, something that would be ordered only once in a while on a hot summer day in the Pacific Northwest.

But James adapted quickly, deciding on which parts of his operation were flexible and which couldn't be changed. He could add biscuits to the morning menu, for example, and could ramp up the iced tea production for those who wanted it—but he would continue to ensure that the coffee beans were extra-fresh and the espresso preparation was just as he had learned back in Seattle. The next time you're in Lexington, stop in for a biscuit and Americano. James and his team will be waiting.

KEY POINTS

· Who are your people? You don't necessarily have to think of them in categories such as age, race, and gender. Instead, you can think of them in terms of shared beliefs and values.

· You can often follow a fad, craze, or trend by establishing yourself as an authority and simplifying something about the process for others hoping to benefit from it.

· Use surveys to understand customers and prospects. The more specific, the better. Ask: "What is the number one thing I can do for you?"

· Use the decision-making matrix to evaluate multiple ideas against one another. You don't have to choose only one idea, but the exercise can help you decide what to pursue next.

PART II

TAKING IT TO THE STREETS

6 • The One-Page Business Plan

IF YOUR MISSION STATEMENT IS MUCH LONGER THAN THIS SENTENCE, IT COULD BE TOO LONG.

> "Plans are only good intentions unless they immediately degenerate into hard work."
>
> —PETER F. DRUCKER

Jen Adrion and Omar Noory graduated from the Columbus (Ohio) College of Art and Design in 2008. They both began freelancing as designers, in addition to Jen teaching at their alma mater and Omar taking a design job at a studio in town. Based in a tiny apartment, they were making ends meet and working jobs related to their degrees, but just one year after graduation, the feeling of burnout from the world of commercial design was inescapable. "Should I have gone to med school?" Jen wondered. "What if accounting would have been a better fit? It was strange to be feeling this way only a year into our careers." On a drive back from Chicago, they talked about other things: an upcoming trip to New York and a plan that they hoped would lead to other travels.

When they got home, Omar looked around for a nice map to help chart their upcoming adventures. Long story short, they couldn't find one that they loved, so they decided to make their own. They stayed up late at night, working on their ideal map while talking about all the places they hoped to visit. When they finished the design, there was just one problem: The printer they wanted to use had a minimum order of fifty units for a cost of $500. It was a lot to spend when they only needed one map, but the project had come to mean more than just a print, so Jen and Omar each put down $250. They loved the final result and hung one of the maps on the wall . . . leaving forty-nine maps with no obvious purpose. They gave a few out to friends . . . and still had forty-four. Finally, Omar asked a crazy question: Would anyone want to *buy* the remaining prints?

They made a one-page website, added a PayPal button, and went to bed. The morning after making their work available for purchase, they woke up to their first sale. Then they made another sale, and then another. Thanks to a surprise mention on a popular design forum, they sold out of their first print run in ten minutes and had tons of messages begging for a reprint. Could this be the answer to designer burnout?

Over the next few months, Jen and Omar introduced more styles and acted on new ideas: a New York City subway map, for example, and a neighborhood-themed map of San Francisco. The plan was to grow steadily but not introduce new products without a valid reason. As good designers, they understood that everything in the store had to be essential. They also understood that although some customers would make more than one purchase, the best way the customers could help was by referring other buyers and fans.

Nine months in, both of them had quit their day jobs to work full-time on the business. "This project has totally restored our passion for design," says Omar. "It feels so liberating to have creative control. It's been an incredible opportunity for us to grow as designers. I feel like our work has progressed more in the past year than it ever has."

Jen and Omar began with an idea, kept costs low, and didn't wait long before stepping forward with a product. Then they adapted to the marketplace response (make more maps!) and built each new product carefully. "It's funny, because we're both obsessive planners," Jen told me. "But this project had almost no planning whatsoever in the beginning, and now it's our full-time work."

The Action Bias

Plan? What plan? Many of our case studies showed a pattern similar to Jen and Omar's: Get started quickly and see what happens. There's nothing wrong with planning, but you can spend a lifetime making a plan that never turns into action. In the battle between planning and action, action wins. Here's how you do it.

SELECT A MARKETABLE IDEA. In Jen and Omar's case, the idea was as follows: *Maybe we're not the only ones who like nice maps. Would other people like them enough to buy one from us?* A marketable idea doesn't have to be a big, groundbreaking idea; it just has to provide a solution to a problem or be useful enough that other people are willing to pay for it. Don't think *innovation*; think *usefulness.**

When you're just getting started, how do you know if an idea is marketable? Well, you don't always know for sure—that's why you start as soon as you can and avoid spending much money. But for more ideas, check out "Seven Steps to Instant Market Testing" on the next page.

---

*I'm grateful to Jason Fried from 37signals for this idea.

Seven Steps to Instant Market Testing*

1. You need to care about the problem you are going to solve, and there has to be a sizable number of other people who also care. Always remember the lesson of convergence: the way your idea intersects with what other people value.

2. Make sure the market is big enough. Test the size by checking the number and relevancy of Google keywords—the same keywords you would use if you were trying to find your product. Think about keywords that people would use to find a solution to a problem. If you were looking for your own product online but didn't know it existed, what keywords would you search for? Pay attention to the top and right sides of the results pages, where the ads are displayed.

3. Focus on eliminating "blatant admitted pain." The product needs to solve a problem that causes pain that the market knows it has. It's easier to sell to someone who knows they have a problem and are convinced they need a solution than it is to persuade someone that they have a problem that needs solving.

4. Almost everything that is being sold is for either a deep pain or a deep desire. For example, people buy luxury items for respect and status, but on a deeper level they want to be loved. Having something that removes pain may be more effective then realizing a desire. You need to show people how you can help remove or reduce pain.

5. Always think in terms of solutions. Make sure your solution is different and better. (Note that it doesn't need to be cheaper—competing on price is usually a losing proposition.) Is the market frustrated with the current solution? Being different isn't enough; differentiation that makes you *better* is what's required. There's no point in introducing something if the market is already satisfied with the

*Parts of this section are based on the advice of Jonathan Fields, the smartest guy I know in market testing. Learn more at JonathanFields.com.

solution—your solution must be different or better. It's significance, not size, that matters.

6. Ask others about the idea but make sure the people you ask are your potential target market. Others may provide insignificant data and are therefore biased and uninformed. Therefore, create a *persona*: the one person who would benefit the most from your idea. Examine your whole network—community, friends, family, social networks—and ask yourself if any of these people match your persona. Take your idea to this person and discuss it with him or her in detail. This will get you much more relevant data than talking to just anyone.

7. Create an outline for what you are doing and show it to a subgroup of your community. Ask them to test it for free in return for feedback and confidentiality. As a bonus, the subgroup feels involved and will act as evangelists. Giving builds trust and value and also gives you an opportunity to offer the whole solution. Use a blog to build authority and expertise on a subject. Leave comments on blogs where your target audience hangs out.

KEEP COSTS LOW. By investing sweat equity instead of money in your project, you'll avoid going into debt and minimize the impact of failure if it doesn't work out. Jen and Omar started with a total budget of exactly $500. In another part of Columbus, Ohio, Amy Turn Sharp runs a handcrafted toy company. Startup cost: $300. Nicolas Luff in Vancouver, Canada, started with only $56.33, the cost of a business license in 2000. In New York City, Michael Trainer started a documentary business for $2,500, the cost of a camera—which he later sold for a profit.

Most of these people are *solopreneurs,* running a light operation by design. But larger businesses with multiple employees also opted to keep the initial costs as low as possible. David Henzell, the agency founder in the United Kingdom whom we met in Chapter 1, started his new partnership for $4,000. Scott Meyer and a business partner, whom we'll hear more about in Chapter 9, started a South Dakota media firm with four employees for under $10,000. The point is that the numbers may vary, but wherever possible, keep costs low.

GET THE FIRST SALE AS SOON AS POSSIBLE. In Louisville, Kentucky, I talked with Nick Gatens, who told me about a small photography project he was working on. Nick worked full-time in information technology for someone else's business and had been trying to break into doing something on his own for a while. The "something" wasn't working yet, though. "I'm not sure I've got the right site design or the right message for visitors," he told me in the coffee shop where we met.

I'm always curious about other people's projects, so I flipped open my laptop and asked for the URL to take a look. "Well," said Nick, "I don't actually have the site up yet."

I'd love to tell you that I gave him some brilliant advice, but I didn't have to say anything at all. Nick stared down at his coffee cup in realization of the obvious: For the project to be successful, he needed to get started. The other people we were hanging out with encouraged him too, and he left the coffee shop determined to make progress quickly.

I was in Kentucky that day on a fifty-state book tour, and when I made it to West Virginia a few weeks later, I saw Nick again. This time, he had an excited look on his face and an important update: "I got the site up, and I made a sale!" A stranger had followed a link from somewhere on the Internet and paid Nick $50 for a print. If you've never sold anything of your own before, you may wonder, *What's the big deal? He sold one $50 print.* But I understood immediately: The first time you make a sale in a new business, no matter the amount, it's a very big deal.

In the weeks between Kentucky and West Virginia, Nick had figured out the real culprit behind his delay. "That conversation made me think about why the site wasn't up yet," he said. "In my head, it was all technical: I had to tweak the design and fix some errors in the code. But being honest with myself, I realized it was really that my fear was still holding me back; the technical stuff was just an excuse. What if I don't sell any prints, or what if nobody likes my work? After realizing why I was stuck, I went home and made the site public that same evening. Within two weeks, I had sold that first print."

Other interviewees told countless versions of this story—about how hard it was to get started but how rewarding it was to receive that first sale. "Once the first sale came in, I *knew* I'd succeed," someone said. "It may not have been completely rational, but that single sale motivated me to take the business much more seriously."

"I was doing a live presentation and opened the shopping cart for our first product launch," someone else said. "I saw orders coming in and literally said out loud, 'Yes, this is it!' It was huge for my momentum at the time."

Therefore, the question you need to ask is . . . how can I get my first sale? Competition from other businesses is a problem for another day; the greater problem you face is inertia. Nick won the battle against inertia by getting his site up and running, and was rewarded with the sale.

MARKET BEFORE MANUFACTURING. It's good to know if people want what you have to offer before you put a lot of work into making it. One way you can do this is through surveys, as we saw in the last chapter—but if you're adventurous, you can also just put something out there, see what the response is, and then figure out how to make it.

A friend of mine did this with an information product aimed at the high-end car industry. He offered a specialty guide that sold for $900 . . . except he didn't actually create it before he advertised it in a magazine. He knew it would be a lot of work to put together the guide, so why do the work if no one wanted it?

Partly to his surprise, he received two orders. The cost of the ad was just $300, so that represented a $1,500 profit if he could actually create the guide. He wrote to the two buyers and said he was developing a new and improved "2.0 version" of the guide and would love to send it to them at no additional charge as long as they could wait thirty days for it to be finished.

Of course, he offered to refund their money if they didn't want to wait, but both buyers chose to wait for the 2.0 version. He then spent the next month frantically writing the guide before sending it to the eagerly waiting customers. Since he knew he had a success on his hands (and it helped that he actually had a product now), he placed another ad and sold ten more over the next few months.

Maybe you won't do it that way, but make sure there is sufficient demand for your product or service before spending your whole life working on it. That's why it's so important to get started as quickly as possible and why the first sale can be so empowering.

RESPOND TO INITIAL RESULTS. After an initial success, regroup and decide what needs to be done next. Jen and Omar responded to demand by adding more maps and carefully creating new products. One year in, they made the decision to stop doing their own fulfillment. "Going to the post office was fun when we were first getting started," Jen said. "But then we had to do it three to five times a week, and it got old." They decided to subcontract their shipping to a local warehouse and ended up saving several hours a week.

Decisions like these may sound like a no-brainer (Why should two designers spend their time making post office runs?), but implementing them can take a lot of work. In Jen and Omar's case, it wasn't just a matter of hiring the local warehouse to do their shipping; they also had to complete the daunting task of syncing their online shopping cart with the fulfillment house.

Finally, it's good to pay attention to what created the initial success even if it seems accidental or coincidental. In Jen and Omar's case, it may have been a fluke the first time they were featured on a major design site, but what if they could make that happen again? It *did* happen again, over and over, because they built relationships and pitched their new projects in a low-key, commonsense manner. This is a process we'll look at more in the next section of the book.

In a microbusiness built on low costs and quick action, you don't need to do much formal planning. Mostly, you need the elements we've discussed throughout the book: a product or service, a group of customers, and a way to get paid. Check out the One-Page Business Plan template on page 102 for a helpful tool.

Freely Receive, Freely Give

As you think through the questions of freedom and value, the most important one is, "How will this business help people?" This isn't simply about being generous, because as a business helps people, the business owner gets paid. Some people design an entire for-profit business around the social component, others shift to focus on it as they go along, and still others integrate a social project within a for-profit business.

Apartheid came to an end in South Africa in 1994, ending

The One-Page Business Plan*

Answer each question with one or two short sentences.

OVERVIEW

What will you sell? _____

Who will buy it? _____

How will your business idea help people? _____

KA-CHING

What will you charge? _____

How will you get paid? _____

How else will you make money from this project? _____

HUSTLING

How will customers learn about your business? _____

How can you encourage referrals? _____

SUCCESS

The project will be successful when it achieves these metrics:

Number of customers _____ *or*

Annual net income _____

(or other metric)

OBSTACLES / CHALLENGES / OPEN QUESTIONS

Specific concern or question #1 _____

Proposed solution to concern #1_____

*You can download or print a free copy of your own customized plan at 100startup
.com. Other helpful, alternative business planning guides are offered by Jim Horan and
Tim Berry.

Specific concern or question #2 _____

Proposed solution to concern #2_____

Specific concern or question #3 _____

Proposed solution to concern #3_____

Deadline: I will launch this project into the world no later than _____.

---

nearly half a century of white-only rule in Africa's most economi-
cally developed country. Nelson Mandela was elected the first black
president the same year, and the country began a slow process of
creating true equality for its "rainbow nation" of people. In addition
to the negative association of apartheid, South Africa was known
for many good things, one of which was its popular prize-winning
wine. The wine region of the Western Cape is older than California's. South Africa provided the royal courts of Europe with wine
for over 350 years, and South African vines were used to start the
Australian wine industry in 1781.

Yet because of apartheid, the $3 billion wine industry had less
than 2 percent black ownership despite the fact that blacks represented 80 percent of the country's population. Enter Khary and
Selena Cuffe, a husband-and-wife team from the United States
who found a way to create a highly profitable business that supports
black vineyard owners in South Africa. Selena, the CEO, explains
it like this: "This venture merges my passion for entrepreneurship
with social justice. The greatest benefit is that my personal and business goals are identical: positively changing people's perception of
the African continent and helping to reinstill a sense of family and
connectivity into the lives of the people that our business touches."

In Tel Aviv, Israel, Daniel Nissimyan founded a paintball

distributor called Matix Ltd. The business stood out to me because of his unique client base: "We sell extreme sports equipment to enthusiasts in Israel and neighboring countries, and also to the Israeli defense establishment for training purposes." Despite the sudden appearance of a number of competitors that sprang up in response to the growth of paintball in Israel, business was good. Matix Ltd. was clearing six figures in income and had sewn up exclusivity contracts with key suppliers, thus thwarting the new competitors.

Daniel went back and forth between Israel and the U.S., and his previous venture was a non-profit that taught karate to children with developmental disabilities in Southern California. Paintball was fun, but Daniel wanted something that combined the non-profit model he started in California with the sports business he ran in Tel Aviv. He found the answer in a new venture called Green Collar, a project that will reduce landfill waste inefficiency while also tapping an overlooked energy source. The goal is to work with municipal governments in both Israel and the Palestinian Authority in an effort to solve common problems and advance joint interests. Here's what Daniel has to say:

> Much more than with Matix [the paintball business], I wake in the morning feeling I'm making the world a better place, and that I don't need to suffer for it. I don't need to volunteer my time to another NGO or donate money; I instead have focused my best efforts to make the world a better place for my country and my children—and I will also be compensated for it.

Whether you follow Daniel's model of designing a business around a social cause (and being paid for it) or find a way to incorporate a community project into your existing business, many entrepreneurs find this to be a critical, fulfilling part of their work.

The 140-Character Mission Statement

Let's break down the planning process into a very simple exercise: defining the mission statement for your business (or your business idea) in 140 characters or less. That is the maximum amount of text for an update on Twitter and a good natural limit for narrowing down a concept. It may help to think of the first two characteristics of any business: a product or service and the group of people who pay for it. Put the two together and you've got a mission statement:

We provide [product or service] for [customers].

As described in Chapter 2, it's usually better to highlight a core benefit of your business instead of a descriptive feature. Accordingly, you can revise the statement a bit to read like this:

We help [customers] do/achieve/other verb [primary benefit].

Focusing like this helps you avoid "corporate speak" and drill down to the real purpose of the business as it relates to your customers. Here are a few examples:

If you have a dog-walking service, the feature is "I walk dogs." The benefit is "I help busy owners feel at ease about their dogs when they're not able to be with them."

If you sell knitted hat patterns, the benefit is something like "I help people be creative by making a hat for themselves or someone close to them."

If you make custom wedding stationery, you might say, "I help couples feel special about their big day by providing them with amazing invitations."

How about you? What is the 140-character (or less) mission statement of your business idea?

Jen and Omar followed the $100 Startup model: Focusing on the specific combination of their unique skills, they made an interesting product that other people also valued. They gave their customers what they wanted without hiding their real lives: Their website contains blog entries on their home life, complete with cat photos—but doesn't go into all the details of making prints that most customers would find irrelevant.

They chose a marketable idea and were encouraged by their first day of sales. They kept costs low, bootstrapping out of their tiny apartment and not borrowing a single dollar. As the business grew rapidly, they regrouped, taking stock of what was working (make more maps) and what wasn't (stop going to the post office all the time).

Most important, instead of thinking about it forever or filling up a binder with projections, Jen and Omar took action.

KEY POINTS

- "Plan as you go" to respond to the changing needs of your customers but launch your business as soon as possible, with a bias toward action.

- Nick's first print sale provided far more motivation than the $50 he received. As soon as possible, find a way to get your first sale.

- Follow the Seven Steps to Instant Market Testing (or the market before manufacturing method) to gauge the initial response.

- Use the One-Page Business Plan to outline your business ideas quickly.

- To avoid overcomplicating things, explain your business with a 140-Character Mission Statement.

THE STEP-BY-STEP GUIDE TO CREATING A KILLER OFFER.

"I have nothing to offer but blood, toil, tears, and sweat."
—WINSTON CHURCHILL

Scott McMurren sat in his office at a TV station in Anchorage, Alaska, looking out at Mount McKinley. The day job was in media sales, where he knocked on doors around town, recruiting advertisers for the station. He also hosted a travel show, something he enjoyed but didn't expect to lead to a full-time gig. Gary Blakely, a buddy of Scott's, had been pestering him for a while about a business idea, but Scott wasn't into it. When two years of Gary's hammering merged with Scott's fatigue from doing the same thing every day, he finally gave in and said, "OK, let's give it a try."

The idea was to create coupon books for independent travelers coming to Alaska. Every year, more than a million visitors show up on the state's doorstep, eager to see Denali National Park and other attractions. Some tourists arrive on cruise ships or guided tours, but many more put together their own trip. As is often the case, the consumer problem and the business opportunity are related: Alaska is a nice place during the summer, but costs are always high. Almost everything in the state is more expensive than the rest of the U.S. to start with, and some travel companies charge even higher prices to visitors. (A common joke is "Welcome to Alaska . . . please hand over your wallet.") The coupon book would be an antidote to high prices, but it would have to provide real value instead of offering the typical, minor discounts available elsewhere.

That's where Scott came in. Since he already had the state contacts through his day job in media sales, all he had to do was get them to commit to a discounted offer, typically a two-for-one deal in which the second night or second person was free. A natural salesman, Scott positioned every deal to grow into another one. When he encountered resistance from a vendor who was reluctant to discount, Scott pointed out that other companies were going along without objection. The implied message was, "Everyone else is doing this. You don't want to be left out."

Once they had proved the benefit to the vendors, the next step was to prove it to the people who would buy the coupon books. You might think Scott and Gary would price the books low to sell as many as possible (comparable products in other places sold for $20 to $25, usually supported by advertising or kickbacks from the vendors), but they had a better idea: price the books at $99.95 and make the value proposition extremely clear. The books contained deals for helicopter flights and tours that cost as much as several hundred dollars, as well as hotels that retailed at more than $100 a night. Why *wouldn't* people pay $99.95 for a product like that?

It was the ultimate follow-your-passion business, combined with a perfect transfer of skills from a job to a microbusiness. Scott had the insider knowledge about the local travel industry, along with a way to leverage the deals to ensure they were all high value. Gary was the production guy, handling everything associated with getting the product together in addition to all the Internet work and the banking. For fifteen years and counting, the TourSaver coupon books have been their primary business and source of income.

• • •

Why is the TourSaver offer so compelling? Because it delivers immediate benefits superior to its cost, with an attractive pitch: "Buy this coupon book, use it once, get your money back. Then you have more than a hundred other uses as a bonus." Scott frames it like this: "Just do the math! Using a single one of the 130+ coupons in the book will save you more than the cost of the book itself."

Another way to think of it is like this: Scott and Gary created an offer you can't refuse. If you were traveling to Alaska and planned to enjoy some kind of sight-seeing opportunity, there's almost no reason why you wouldn't want one of their books.

The Orange and the Donut

A few years ago, I ran my first marathon in Seattle. I'd love to tell you I ran strong to the finish, but by mile 18 I was wiped out, focusing entirely on putting one foot in front of the other. As I trudged along in the final hour, I spotted a volunteer handing out fresh orange slices on the side of the road ahead of me. Tired as I was, I made sure to change my position, slow down, and gratefully accept the gift. The piece of fresh orange was an offer I couldn't refuse—even though it was free, I would have gladly paid for it if I had the money and was in the right frame of mind to make a transaction.

Two miles ahead, I saw another volunteer handing out a different gift: halves of Krispy Kreme donuts. Unfortunately, this offer did not excite me (or any other runners I saw) at all. I'm no puritan and have eaten more than my share of donuts over the years, but three hours into the longest race of my life was bad timing for a sugar rush. The offer was unattractive and a poor fit for the context.*

---

*Ironically, there were no donuts available *after* the 26.2-mile race, something many runners would have been thrilled to see. Keep this in mind if you are ever in charge of providing donuts for marathoners.

A compelling offer is like a slice of orange at mile 18. It's a marriage proposal from the guy or girl you've been waiting for your whole life. An offer you can't refuse is like the $20,000 Bonderman Fellowship offered every year to graduating seniors at the University of Washington. The fellowship has very strict rules: Take our money in cash and travel the world on your own; don't come back for eight months. Oh, and once in a while send us a quick note so we can tell your parents you're alive. If you guessed that hundreds of students compete for the fellowship every year, you'd be right.

How can you construct an offer that your prospects won't refuse? Remember, first you need to sell what people want to buy—give them the fish. Then make sure you're marketing to the right people at the right time. Sometimes you can have the right crowd at the wrong time; marathon runners are happy to eat donuts after the race, but not at mile 18. Then you take your product or service and craft it into a compelling pitch . . . an offer they can't refuse.

Here's how you do it.

1. Understand that what we want and what we say we want are not always the same thing.

The next time you get on a crowded plane and head to your cramped middle seat in the back, with a screaming infant seated behind you at no extra charge, remember this principle. For years travelers have been complaining about crowded planes and cramped seats, and for years airlines have been ignoring them. Every once in a while, an airline creates a campaign to respond to the concern: "We're giving more legroom in coach!"

It sounds great, but a few months later they inevitably reverse course and remove the extra inches of space. Why? Because despite what they say, most travelers don't value the extra legroom enough to pay for it; instead, they value the lowest-priced flights above any other concerns. Airlines have figured this out, so they give people what they want—not what they say they want. A good offer has to be what people *actually* want and are willing to pay for.

2. Most of us like to buy, but we don't usually like to be sold.

An offer you can't refuse may apply subtle pressure, but nobody likes a hard sell. Instead, compelling offers often create an illusion that a purchase is an invitation, not a pitch. Social shopping services such as Groupon (see Chapter 8) and Living Social have been successful in recruiting their customers to do most of their marketing for them. Indeed, the biggest complaint about these businesses is often that they sell out of deals too quickly, also known as "They won't let me give them my money!"

As you might imagine, the path of least resistance is a good place to stand. Visitors to Alaska quickly understand why a $100 coupon book is worth much more than $100. Marathon runners do not need to be sold on the benefits of fresh oranges after three hours of running. Adventurous college students will grasp the value of a $20,000 "go travel somewhere and do what you want" fellowship without much explaining.

Offer Construction Project
**MAGIC FORMULA: THE RIGHT AUDIENCE,
THE RIGHT PROMISE, THE RIGHT TIME =
OFFER YOU CAN'T REFUSE**

BASICS

What are you selling? _____

How much does it cost? _____

Who will take immediate action on this offer? _____

BENEFITS

The primary benefit is _____

An important secondary benefit is _____

OBJECTIONS

What are the main objections to the offer?

1.

2.

3.

How will you counter these objections?

1.

2.

3.

TIMELINESS

Why should someone buy this now?

What can I add to make this offer even more compelling?

---

3. Provide a nudge.

The very best offers create a "You must have this right now!" feeling among consumers, but many other offers can succeed by creating a less immediate sense of urgency. Providing a gentle nudge to encourage immediate action separates a decent offer from a high-performing one. Let's look at a few examples.

EXAMPLE 1: THE YOGA STUDIO

Jonathan Fields, a hedge fund lawyer turned fitness entrepreneur, owned a Manhattan yoga studio that sought to be at the top of the market. A single class cost $18, and membership cost $119 a month. Toward the end of summer, the studio saw a significant drop-off in business, but when October rolled around, people got back to their routine and started coming in more often.

Jonathan wanted to find a way to inspire people to come back earlier than expected and get as much commitment from them as possible. He had an idea for an offer they couldn't refuse: Starting September 1, first-time members could get unlimited classes through the end of the year for $180. This was essentially four months of yoga for the price of 45 days, or 62 percent off the normal price. Two additional factors were added to make it even more interesting: First, the sooner a new member signed up, the more classes he or she could attend, thus creating instant urgency. Second, the offer could be withdrawn at any time; if someone came in on September 3 and wasn't sure about committing to the rest of the year, the staff made sure to let that person know that the offer might not be available later in the week.

Thanks to New Year's resolutions, most fitness centers take in the bulk of their new members in January. Jonathan's strategy helped his business gain a big increase in September, traditionally a difficult month. Also, September was close enough to January that by the time the new year rolled around, many of the members were committed enough to transfer to a monthly plan—at the regular price.

EXAMPLE 2: THE INEFFICIENT BUSINESS MODEL
(MARKET INEFFICIENCY = BUSINESS OPPORTUNITY)

Whenever something is more complicated than it should be or any time you spot an inefficiency in the market, you can also find a good business idea. Priceline.com took advantage of hotel inefficiencies by creating a system that allowed consumers to book rooms at name-brand hotels for much less than the retail rates. Then other companies took advantage of Priceline's lack of transparency by creating a business model that allows travelers to know which hotels Priceline works with. Each of these models includes a compelling offer:

> Priceline's compelling offer: Save 40 percent or more on name-brand hotels, guaranteed.
>
> Third-party compelling offer: Learn exactly which hotel you'll get with Priceline . . . and save even more when you know exactly how much to bid.

You can also derive a powerful business model from traditional systems that lack transparency. If you want to make a traditional real estate agent mad, ask the agent about Redfin, the Seattle-based service that splits commissions with home buyers. I learned this lesson when one agent told me that Redfin "should be illegal" and that I was doing a disservice to hardworking people by endorsing it. Why are (some) agents so testy, and why should it be illegal to save consumers money? Oh, because the money is coming from the pockets of real estate agents, who are used to receiving full, hefty commissions regardless of the amount of work they perform. Redfin has succeeded by challenging gatekeepers and addressing a huge inefficiency in the marketplace.

Speaking of home owners, the DirectBuy franchise was started in order to offer "ordinary people" (i.e., non-contractors) access to retailer pricing on appliances and home electronics. To get around the concerns of retailers and manufacturers, DirectBuy structured its business model on charging a flat fee for consumers to join. The compelling offer is: Invest in our membership, and you'll save thousands on home remodeling.*

---

*Unfortunately, the fee to join DirectBuy is thousands of dollars, and it's not always clear how much money the average home owner will save with the service. But as with Priceline, perhaps this creates an opportunity for another third-party business to provide the information.

EXAMPLE 3: THE GRAPHIC FACILITATOR

I'll invite you to meet Brandy Agerbeck in these pages, but you can "meet" her first by examining the mindmap she made for us below.*

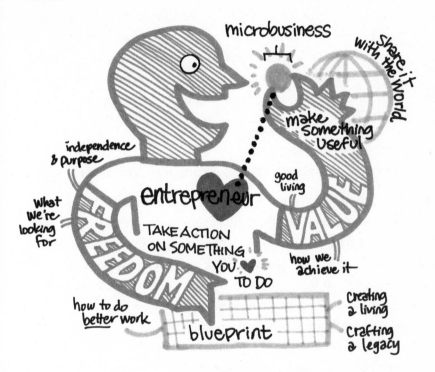

Brandy runs a business of one, with the philosophy "never have a boss, never be a boss." Creating graphical representations of ideas—usually those expressed in meetings, retreats, or conferences—is Brandy's full-time work. Over the last fifteen years, she's worked with hundreds of clients at all kinds of events. It's a beautiful business model from a talented artist, but it also raises a question: How do you nudge or win over executives who don't get it at first?

*To watch a short video on how Brandy creates her great work, check out YouTube.com/loosetoothdotcom.

From countless interactions about the valuable service she provides, here's what Brandy learned. She starts every initial conversation by saying, "I have a fantastic, strange job." This creates curiosity and also serves to make the other person not feel bad if he or she is unfamiliar with the world of graphic facilitation. Next, Brandy learned that her target market may be the executives or meeting leaders she serves, but they aren't necessarily the ones who hire her. "I am most often hired by facilitators, acting as their visual silent partners," she says. "They can focus entirely on their client knowing their process, and progress is documented."

Perceived Value and the Expensive Starbucks Run

After nearing the end of a five-hour drive from Boise to Salt Lake City, I stopped off at a Starbucks about twenty minutes away from the bookstore I was speaking at that evening. On the way inside, I grabbed something from the trunk and left the keys inside. Nice move, Chris. It was even worse because I didn't realize my mistake until I had finished my latte and email session an hour later, shortly before I was due to arrive at the bookstore.

I was mad at myself for being so stupid, but I had to think quickly. Using a combination of technology (iPod touch, MiFi, cell phone), I located the number of a local locksmith and quickly rang him up. "Uh, can you please come as soon as possible?" He agreed to be as fast as he could.

Much to my surprise, the locksmith pulled up in a van just three minutes later. Impressive, right? Then he got out his tools and approached the passenger door. In less than ten seconds, he had the door open, allowing me to retrieve my keys from the trunk and get on with my life. "How much do I owe you?" I asked. Perhaps it's because I don't own a car and the last time I paid a locksmith was ten years ago, or maybe I'm just cheap, but for whatever reason I expected him to ask for something like $20. Instead, he said, "That will be $50, please."

I hadn't discussed the price with him before he came out and was in no position to negotiate, so I gave him the cash and thanked him. But something was unsettling about the transaction, and I tried to figure out what it was. I was mad at myself for locking my keys in the car—it was obviously no one's fault but my own—but I also felt that $50 was too much to pay for such a brief service.

As I drove away, I realized that I secretly wanted him to take longer in getting to me, even though that would have delayed me further. I wanted him to struggle with unlocking my car as part of a major effort, even though that made no sense whatsoever. The locksmith met my need and provided a quick, comprehensive solution to my problem. I was unhappy about our exchange for no good reason.

Mulling it over, I realized that the way we make purchasing decisions isn't always rational. I thought back to something that had happened in the early days of my business. I had produced a twenty-five-page report on booking discount airfare and sold it for $25. Many people bought it, but others complained: *Twenty-five pages for $25? That's too expensive.*

I knew I couldn't please everyone, but I didn't understand this specific objection. The point of the report was to help people save money on plane tickets, and many readers reported saving $300 or more after one quick read. "What does the length of the report have to do with the price?" I remember thinking about that one complaint. "If I gave you a treasure map, would you complain that it was only one page long?" It turned out the joke was on me. All of us place a subjective value on goods or services that may not relate to what they "should" be.

Just as what we want and what we say we want aren't always

the same thing, the way we place a value on something isn't always rational. You must learn to think about value the way your customers do, not necessarily the way you would like them to.

Compelling Offer Tool Kit:
FAQ, Guarantee, and Overdelivery

As you continue to work on your offer, three tools will assist you in making it more compelling: the FAQ page (or wherever you provide the answers to common questions), an incredible guarantee, and giving your customers more than they expect. Let's look at each of them in detail.

1. Frequently Asked Questions, AKA "What I Want You to Know"

You might think that a frequently asked questions (FAQ) page is designed merely to answer questions. Surprise! It's not . . . or at least, that's not its only function. A well-designed FAQ page also has another, extremely important purpose. You could call it "operation objection busting": The additional purpose of a FAQ is to provide reassurance to potential buyers and overcome objections. Your mission, should you choose to accept it, is to identify the main objections your buyers will have when considering your offer and carefully respond to them *in advance*.

Wondering what the objections to your offer will be? They fall into two categories: general and specific. The specific objections relate to an individual product or service, so it's hard to predict what they might be without looking at a particular offer. General objections, however, come up with almost any purchase, so that's what we'll look at here. These objections usually relate to very basic human desires, needs, concerns, and fears. Here are a few common ones:

- How do I know this really works?
- I don't know if this is a good investment (and/or I'm not sure I have the money to spare).
- I'm not sure I can trust you with my money.
- What do other people think about this offer?
- I wonder if I can find this information/get this product or service without paying.
- I worry about sharing my information online (or another privacy concern).

The core concern for each of these objections relates to *trust* and *authority*. You must create consumer confidence in order to overcome the objections. As you craft the offer, think about the objections . . . and then flip them around in your favor. You want to send messages like these:

- This really works because . . .
- This is a great investment because . . .
- You can trust us with your money because . . . (alternatively, You don't have to trust us with your money, because we work with an established, trusted third party . . .)
- Other people think this is great, and here's what they say . . .
- You have to pay to get this product or service (alternatively, The free versions aren't as good, it takes a lot of work to get it on your own, etc.)
- Your information and privacy are 100 percent secure because . . .

See how it works? The point is not to be defensive (you want to avoid that) but rather to be proactive in responding to concerns. One model you can use when describing your offer is outlined below in what we'll call a "rough awesome format." It works like this:

> Point 1: This thing is so awesome! [primary benefit]
>
> Point 2: Seriously, it's really awesome. [secondary benefit]
>
> Point 3: By the way, you don't need to worry about anything. [response to concerns]
>
> Point 4: See, it's really awesome. What are you waiting for? [take action]

In the rough awesome format, point 1 is the main benefit, point 2 is a reinforcement of the main benefit or an important side benefit, point 3 is where you deal with the objections, and point 4 is where you bring it all together and nudge buyers toward a call to action. You won't always get it right at first—sometimes you'll discover additional objections as you go through the initial sales process with real-time customers—but dealing with the most important objections from the beginning will help you get off to a much better start than the wait-and-see approach.

2. The Incredible Guarantee, AKA "Don't Be Afraid"

Regardless of what you're selling, the overriding concern of many potential customers is, "What if I don't like it? Can I get my money back?" A common and highly effective way to combat this concern is to offer a satisfaction guarantee. A word of advice: Do not make your guarantee complicated, confusing, or boring. You don't want your customer to overthink it! Keep it simple and easy.

Further, if there is any way you can tie the promised results of your offer to the guarantee, do so. Nev Lapwood, who runs a snowboarding instruction program you'll read about in Chapter 11, offers a 120 percent guarantee. If the program doesn't rock your world, you'll get 100 percent of your money back, *plus* 20 percent for your trouble.* When I developed the Travel Hacking Cartel, I promised that members who applied the program's strategies would earn at least 100,000 frequent flyer miles a year, enough for four free plane tickets.

Not every business will be able to offer an incredible guarantee, especially if there are substantial up-front costs for delivery. Alternatively, you can also make the deliberate choice *not* to guarantee your product or service and then make a big deal about that fact. The lack of a guarantee can then act as a filtering process, gently steering away customers who weren't a good fit, while reinforcing the purchase for those who are.

Generally, you should offer an incredible guarantee or no guarantee at all. A weak guarantee, or one that is unclear, can work against your credibility instead of helping it.

3. Overdelivering, AKA "Wow, Look at All This Extra Stuff I Didn't Expect"

Immediately after buying something, we often experience a pang of anxiety: Was this a good purchase? Did I waste my money? You'll want to get out in front of this feeling by making people feel good about the action they just took. The easiest and most critical way to reinforce their decision is by giving them quick access to what they paid for. But to go further, you'll want to *overdeliver*: give

---

*I asked Nev if he's had issues with customers abusing this policy. His response: Nope, no problems at all. Nev credits Tim Ferriss, author of *The Four-Hour Workweek*, with giving him this idea.

them more than they expected. You can do this by upgrading their purchase unexpectedly by sending a handwritten thank-you card in the mail or in whatever way makes the most sense for your business.

The point is that the small things count.

Like the orange slice at mile 18 of the marathon, an offer you can't refuse comes along at just the right time. As you follow your blueprint to freedom, think carefully about how you can create a similarly compelling offer.

The next step is to take the offer out into the world. Ready?

KEY POINTS

· As much as possible, connect your offer to the direct benefits customers will receive. Like the Alaska coupon books, a compelling offer pays for itself by making a clear value proposition.

· What people want and what they say they want are not always the same thing; your job is to figure out the difference.

· When developing an offer, think carefully about the objections and then respond to them in advance.

· Provide a nudge to customers by getting them to make a decision. The difference between a good offer and a great offer is *urgency* (also known as timeliness): Why should people act *now*?

· Offer reassurance and acknowledgment immediately after someone buys something or hires you. Then find a small but meaningful way to go above and beyond their expectations.

A TRIP TO HOLLYWOOD FROM YOUR LIVING ROOM OR THE CORNER COFFEE SHOP.

"Before beginning, prepare carefully."
—MARCUS TULLIUS CICERO

Let's take a trip to Hollywood, by way of our local cinema or movie theater. Every year, a number of blockbuster films come out that cost a huge amount of money to produce, often $100 million or more. Studio executives know they have only a limited window to ensure a big hit. If the opening weekend isn't huge, they may still have a good movie, but not the blockbuster they need to recoup their high costs.

The executives also know that although some people don't decide which movie they want to see until they get to the theater, lots of other people go to see a particular movie. If they've been hearing about it in advance, building up their anticipation and getting excited, they're all the more eager to see the movie—and tell their friends about it too.

This is why Hollywood begins the "pre-launch" for a big film many months in advance, often a whole season or even an entire year in advance for the right film. During this time they are showing previews at the beginning of other movies, building buzz through an Internet campaign, and working the PR angles far in advance of the movie actually coming out.

The pre-launch campaign is a success when people eagerly await the film, complaining about how long it takes to arrive, until the day—"finally"—it's ready to be screened for the public. Then, the studio hopes, hundreds of thousands of filmgoers will pay their money and stream into the theater. Without an active pre-launch campaign, the movie may be great but the odds of commercial success are far lower.

The same principle holds true for microbusinesses. Whether a Hollywood movie or the debut of your new sock-knitting class, launches are built primarily through a series of regular communications with prospects and existing customers. Just like the movie executives who release trailers over time (first a short one, then a longer one) and the press events that Apple built up over time with Steve Jobs at the helm (building anticipation for future products to a fever pitch), small businesses can reproduce this cycle in their own way.*

• • •

Karol Gajda and Adam Baker, two friends with separate businesses in different parts of the country, decided to team up for a big project. Karol had completed an engineering degree from the University of Michigan, but never actually worked as an engineer. He first had the idea from reading a classic ninety-year-old marketing book called *Scientific Advertising* by Claude Hopkins. In the book, Hopkins discussed "fire sales"—the old-school, "everything must go" tactic used by furniture stores for decades. Karol didn't have a furniture store, but he wondered . . . What if we put together a modern-day fire sale, with an emphasis on giving away a ton of value for a low price, but only for a limited time?

*Any analysis of "launch marketing" should give credit to the classic book *Influence* by Robert Cialdini, who was one of the first to study how consumers decide to make purchasing decisions. Jeff Walker, an entrepreneur and educator, is also well known for his work on product launches.

Karol and Adam were both in the information publishing business, and they quickly went to work, approaching other colleagues
to participate. The pitch was intriguing: Contribute your products
to the overall mix to be sold as a group for a low price and during
a limited time. Oh, and if you help promote the offer to your own
audience of customers and followers, you'll earn an 80 percent commission on everything you sell. It was a good pitch, and Karol and
Adam had spent plenty of time building relationships and developing a strong reputation for their work. Out of twenty-five requests,
twenty-three people said yes.

Packaging everything together, they ended up with a monster
package valued at a retail price of $1,054. They would sell the pack-
age for $97, less than 10 percent of the overall value and a price to
which they expected customers would respond well. The "hook"
came from the fire-sale idea: The offer would be available for only
seventy-two hours—no packages would ever be sold again after the
limited time period.

The big day came, and they put the offer online. For ten minutes
nothing happened. Karol sat looking in anticipation at the stats in
Austin while Adam was biting his nails in Indianapolis. Was something wrong? Fortunately not . . . It turned out they were just ten
minutes early. All of a sudden, a trickle of visitors became a stream,
then a flood, as more and more people heard about the offer and
came by to purchase. *Wham!* The server was hit hard, and Karol's
Gmail account reported "Notification of payment received" over
and over.

The flood continued for the rest of the day, slowed down a bit
on the second day, and then picked back up at the end of the third
and final day. When the smoke cleared, Karol and Adam added up
the results. Total sales: $185,755 in three sleep-deprived days. Such
was the power of a well-crafted product launch.

It Was a Dark and Stormy Night

Because a planned launch campaign can provide far better results than simply putting something out there and saying, "Hey, here you go," you'll want to think carefully about how to structure it. The campaign usually unfolds in a series of messages you send to your audience, and you should keep the Hollywood analogy in mind: The worst thing you could do for a launch is to open your movie without letting anyone know. A much better thing is to tell a story. The story unfolds like this . . .

An early look at the future. In the first mention of your upcoming launch, you don't want to give all the details away; it's usually better to start with a simple heads-up. You want to say something like this: "Hey, I'm working on something interesting. It's going to be a big deal when it's finished, but for now I'm just letting you know that it's coming down the line." The goal is to slowly build anticipation for what eventually will be available for purchase.

Why this project will matter. The most important early message about the launch (and one that has to be reinforced continually) is why your prospects and customers should care. In the blitz of communication that we all process every day, why should anyone stop and pay attention to this project? The message you want to communicate is: "This is why this project will be a game changer, here's how people will benefit, and here's why you should care."

The plan for the big debut. The previous two messages, as well as any others, have been about the project itself, not the actual launch. Here's where you roll out some of the details for the launch itself. When will it be? How will it work? Will there be some kind of bonus for early buyers? Most important, what do people need to know at this time?

Whoa, we're almost ready! This communication happens right before the launch, sometimes as late as the day before. The message is: "This is the calm before the storm. We're coming down to the wire and are really excited about this." Any last-minute reminders or launch details are included here, and the goal is to convert anticipation into an actual decision. (You want prospects to decide in advance that they want what you're putting together.)

OMG, HERE IT IS! The message is: "It's finally here, everyone has been waiting, and now we're ready to go." This communication tends to be shorter than the others because if you've done your job right, many buyers are already prepared to purchase. Here's where you open the gates to the hordes . . . or at least that's what you *hope* will happen. In this message you send them a link (or give them another way to purchase) and encourage them to take action.

INTERLUDE

Let's pause here for a moment. What happens immediately after this point is just as important as what has happened already. A good marketer doesn't rest on her laurels after a launch, because she knows she can probably increase the results significantly with little effort. A launch often results in a response cycle like this:

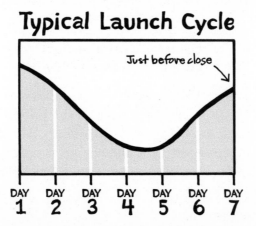

Typical Launch Cycle

If the launch is a week long, you'll tend to see a strong response on the first and second days, followed by a significant downturn and then a big uptick right before the close. This further illustrates why you need a launch cycle: If you have no closing, you won't see the uptick! If you just launch and move on, you'll have no opportunity for growth. Now back to the story . . .

Here's how it's going. Something always goes wrong in every launch. Here's a chance to address or correct it, along with updating everyone on how things are going. During this time, it's also important to share stories of happy customers who have purchased already. The message is, "Look at all these people who are already benefiting from our product."

The clock's a-ticking. Right before the offer goes off the market, or before you remove the bonuses, or before the price goes up, here's where you make one final push. The message is, "It's almost over. Here's your last chance before you lose out."

"I'd like to thank my mother for believing in me." Any good launch has a closing period in which you bring the roller coaster to a stop, even if the offer will still be available in a different form. The message is, "It's all over now. Thanks, everyone. Here's what's coming next."

Disaster and Recovery:
"HORDE OF NEW CUSTOMERS" EDITION

Like the problem of having too much money, having too many customers is usually a good problem to have—but it can still be a tough scramble if the customers all arrive at once and a key supplier isn't ready. Here's what David Wachtendonk, the founder of a party planning business in Chicago, learned when he received two thousand more customers than expected for a promotion.

In June 2010 our company participated in a Groupon. We did some research, and it appeared this could be a good avenue for our company to get some exposure for a new concept we wanted to launch in Chicago. After some discussion with the Groupon guys, we agreed it would be a match made in heaven. Our last remaining task was to find a venue that could support the deal. After some initial opportunities fell through, we found a new restaurant that agreed to work with us.

The day the deal went live, we had no idea what was about to happen. Our Groupon rep estimated we would sell about 1,000 to 1,500 units . . . but 3,300 units later, the day ended. We thought we had systems in place to deal with growth, but unfortunately we became overwhelmed. The phone was off the hook and emails poured in, which we fielded to the best of our ability. Most of the customers were fairly understanding as we were a small business, but not everyone was nice about it.

We found out after the deal had launched that the restaurant was in the middle of rebranding to a sports bar, which is not the ideal situation for a dinner theater. Their clientele changed, the atmosphere was evolving, and the owner of the business did his best to accommodate us. Unfortunately, your best isn't always good enough, and our new customers let us know it. We worked tirelessly with their team to get them up to speed on how to handle large groups and even provided our own on-site hostess and manager for the majority of the shows with the hopes of improving the experience. Due to things out of our control, the quality didn't meet expectations at first—service became sloppy, and the overall experience was diluted. The first few shows were challenging, but over time the experience got better. Forty-seven shows later, we finally wrapped things up.

Our company had done its research and what we thought was adequate due diligence for the deal, but our efforts fell short. We should have been more proactive and done a better job communi-

*cating expectations to our customers. Thankfully, our team made it
through the experience and can live to tell the story. The question
people ask me all the time is, "Would you do another Groupon?"
The honest answer is that I would. Along with the challenges the
Groupon presented, it provided exposure that traditional marketing
never would have achieved.*

As with everything else in life, it's important to keep your word
with launches. If your offer ended at a set time and you had a big
response, you'll invariably be contacted with requests for exceptions after it's over. It's tempting to take more money, but if you
said it would end at a set time, you need to stick to your decision.
In the long run, this works in your favor, because people will realize that you mean what you say. Karol and Adam received numerous requests for their bundled package after the seventy-two-hour
period had ended, but they politely declined each one.

One more thing: If you admit to a flaw, weakness, or limitation
in your product, this will probably help instead of harm you. This
is because when we are evaluating a purchasing decision, we like to
consider both the strengths and the weaknesses. If a product developer personally tells us it's not perfect—"and here's why"—we
tend to trust him or her more.

You can see this style of messaging in President Obama's 2012
reelection campaign. An early ad *in favor* of reelection contained the
following statement from a supporter: "I don't agree with Obama
on everything, but I respect and trust him." Meanwhile, an ad that
launched the same week *against* reelection contained the following
statement from someone who was opposed: "I like Obama, but I
just don't understand his policies."

These are essentially the same statements, flipped around to place the emphasis on what each side wants voters to believe. Each message contains both an admission of uncertainty *and* an argument, thus making both pitches a good fit for independent voters who haven't made up their minds yet.*

In all the messages you send (whether delivered via email or in another way), you'll want to be mindful of several qualities. The first and most important is what we've mentioned already: the need to tell a good story. On its own, however, a good story isn't always enough. You also need to think about "relatability" and timeliness. Relatability, which may or may not be a real word, refers to the need to ensure that the people who hear about the launch can relate to it. Do they see themselves in the characters in your story, and can they clearly understand how it will help them? Do they get it?

The final factor is timeliness, and it can be the critical difference between good results ("We did OK") and great results ("We killed it!"). Without timeliness, customers may evaluate the offer and agree that it's interesting, but fail to take action because there is no need for them to do so right away. You don't want to pressure people into buying if they're not ready, but you do want to instill a sense of urgency. That's why a good launch always factors in a concern for timeliness.

It's Not (All) About the Sales

The goal of a good launch is not just to convert as many prospects as possible; it's also to preserve your relationship with other prospects

---

*In addition to admitting a flaw or weakness, popular launch tactics include giving away a free copy of the product (turning it into a contest in which the aspiring winners compete for it publicly) and showing off a "sneak preview" of the product. Because launches are so important, I've included more tips and tactics in the free resources at 100startup.com.

and increase your influence. The reason this is important is because you don't want to hammer people too hard; it's better to build relationships over time.

Some people will always complain whenever you sell anything at any price. There's nothing you can do about that attitude, so just accept it and don't cater to those people. But you *do* want to pay attention to your broader base. What are they saying about you? How do they perceive the value of your offer and the style of your messaging? A good launch should increase sales and influence at the same time. If you're getting positive feedback from people who don't buy your product but want to support you in other ways, you're on the right track.

Storytelling and the Empire Building Kit Launch

It was my most important launch to date: an online business course called the Empire Building Kit that eventually formed the basis for this book. For months I conducted interviews and research, capturing lessons from unconventional entrepreneurs and extracting the secrets of their success. As I prepared to make it available, though, I felt stuck—something wasn't coming together, and I kept procrastinating on the launch date.

While planning a trip to Europe and West Africa, I had a flight booked that eventually would take me to Chicago but no onward ticket to my home in Portland. On a whim I checked the Amtrak schedule, thinking there was no way I'd want to take a train halfway across the country but I might as well take a look. To my surprise, the name of the Amtrak train from Chicago to Portland was the *Empire Builder.* Hmmm. I began to get an idea, but initially thought it was too crazy to implement. That same evening, the doorbell rang and the UPS guy dropped off a package. When I opened the box, I discovered a free messenger bag sent by some new friends at Tom Bihn's company (profiled in Chapter 13). The name of the bag was . . . *Empire Builder.*

I'm not sure if God, the universe, or Tom Bihn's company was sending me the message, but I decided to follow the idea where it led. I made plans to go to West Africa then fly home via Chicago and launch the Empire Building Kit on a single day, live from the *Empire Builder* train. Oh, and it also happened to be my birthday—so I made that part of the story as well.

I asked my friend J. D. Roth to come along with me, so he and I met up in Chicago and prepared for the journey. Upon embarking on the train, we set up a "blogger's lounge" in the Amtrak viewing car complete with various Apple products—amusing the other passengers, many of whom were elderly sightseers. In the weeks before the big day, I had been telling my community about the plan with a mixture of excitement and dread; I was excited to launch the new course but scared that I wouldn't be able to finish it in time. With so much riding on the story, there was no flexibility on the date and no backup plan if things didn't work out.

Thankfully, everything worked as it should. I finished the final copyedits on my Lufthansa flight to Chicago. Two days later, we launched the Empire Building Kit to hundreds of eager buyers, many of whom had been waiting for it since the pre-launch campaign. The launch cleared over $100,000 in sales before I turned it off exactly twenty-four hours later as our train rolled through Washington State and down into Oregon. The message had a good story and built-in timeliness: Once we hit Portland, the deal was over.

My favorite part was receiving emails from people who said they weren't interested in the course but had been enjoying the story of the train ride. I don't always get it right, but this time everything fell into place.

London Airport Launch, Eleven Hours to Brazil

After finishing a university course, Andreas Kambanis struggled for six months, not wanting to get a real job and trying to build something for himself. The goal was to develop an iPhone app and online guide to London cycling routes, but the initial setbacks were significant. Among other things, Andreas used the name *London Cyclist* before realizing that there already was a publication with that name, triggering an angry letter and the threat of a lawsuit. Meanwhile, all of his friends had gone on to work for companies, so they had money to go out at night while Andreas stayed home.

Andreas stuck it out, planning for his first launch with a partner right before leaving on a personal trip to Brazil. A few weeks before departure, the partner dropped out. Andreas cut back on the expected deliverables but decided to keep going with both the launch and the trip.

The big day came, and he launched the app from the Heathrow airport departure lounge literally thirty minutes before boarding the flight. Settling into economy class for the eleven-hour flight, he had plenty of time to think about his new business, but in the days before in-flight Internet was common, there wasn't anything he could do about it. As he explained later, going offline right after releasing the app probably wasn't the best decision, but without much of an audience, he didn't expect any real results to appear right away. After finally touching down in São Paulo, Andreas couldn't resist activating the roaming feature of his iPhone for a quick check.

Bleary-eyed and sitting in a cramped window seat, he pulled up the numbers and couldn't believe what he saw—a pile of orders was flooding in, just as Karol and Adam had experienced earlier. It wasn't a fortune, but in the time he had been flying across the Atlantic, the launch had paid for his plane ticket and the first week of lodging. Andreas continued on to a connecting flight to Rio, abandoning all hope of not using the roaming option on his phone, and kept watching the sales come through.

I prefer to spend my launches at home with sixteen ounces of coffee in hand, dealing with the inevitable technical glitch while communicating with partners and buyers. But in this case, having the forced deadline of the upcoming flight—and then getting on the plane in Heathrow, ready or not—served as a powerful motivation for Andreas. "It's hard to put into words why the physical deadline was such an important part of getting the project done," he told me. "I think it was so motivational because it seemed impossible to achieve, and it made me kill everything that didn't add to the project being finished."*

• • •

A good launch strategy can help almost any business, online or offline. Let's take a look at how an independent publishing company used the same tactics that worked for Karol and Adam, but for a launch that was completely offline and local. Anastasia Valentine publishes children's books and used to work with "big companies who had gigantic marketing budgets." Naturally, she didn't have access to the same kind of resources for her own launch, but she knew enough to create anticipation over time for a specific event.

The first part was to start with the ask—to ask everyone she knew for help. "We weren't sure how to filter our requests," Anastasia said, "so instead of filtering, we just asked everyone for everything. We asked for newspaper coverage, TV appearances, endorsements, donations for a big party, and anything else we could think of."

The requests paid off when she got a positive response to almost everything. When the big day arrived, the line went out the door, and Anastasia had made sure to create a good experience for the attendees. Since adults who buy children's books usually arrive with kids in tow, she added coloring spaces and a homemade pin-the-tooth-on-the-crocodile contest. Even though the launch was for an

*An unexpected benefit of Andreas's launch trip was meeting someone in South America who would become his longtime girlfriend. Your results may vary!

offline event, Web traffic increased by 267 percent and the mailing list doubled. Learning to ask was also instructive. "People we didn't think would have the slightest interest showed up . . . with friends!" she said. "Meanwhile, people who we thought were totally interested never even responded. The lesson was that you shouldn't assume someone isn't interested or won't attend or won't buy."

If you're just getting started with your own launch planning, check out the Thirty-Nine-Step Product Launch Checklist below. This checklist has two uses: as a template for a new business planning its first launch and as an idea generator for an existing business.

Thirty-Nine-Step Product Launch Checklist

Note: Every product launch is different. Use these steps as a guideline to your own. Often by adding one or two steps you would otherwise leave out, you'll get a significant increase in sales.

THE BIG PICTURE

1. Ensure that your product or service has a clear value proposition.* What do customers receive when exchanging money for your offer?

2. Decide on bonuses, incentives, or rewards for early buyers. How will they be rewarded for taking action?

3. Have you made the launch fun somehow? (Remember to think about non-buyers as well as buyers. If people don't want to buy, will they still enjoy hearing or reading about the launch?)

4. If your launch is online, have you recorded a video or audio message to complement the written copy?

*This is superimportant! USP means "unique selling proposition" and refers to the one thing that distinguishes your offering from all others. Why should people pay attention to what you are selling? You must answer this question well.

---

5. Have you built anticipation into the launch? Are prospects excited?

6. Have you built *urgency*—not the false kind but a real reason for timeliness—into the launch?

7. Publish the time and date of the launch in advance (if it's online, some people will be camped out on the site an hour before, hitting the refresh button every few minutes).

8. Proofread all sales materials multiple times . . . and get someone else to review them as well.

9. Check all Web links in your shopping cart or payment processor, and then double-check them from a different computer with a different browser.

NEXT STEPS

10. If this is an online product, is it properly set up in your shopping cart or with PayPal?

11. Test every step of the order process repeatedly. Whenever you change any variable (price, order components, text, etc.), test it again.

12. Have you registered all the domains associated with your product? (Domains are cheap; you might as well get the .com, .net, .org, and any very similar name if available.)

13. Are all files uploaded and in the right place?

14. Review the order page carefully for errors or easy-to-make improvements. Print it out and share it with several friends for review, including a couple of people who don't know anything about your business.

15. Read important communications (launch message, order page, sales page) out loud. You'll probably notice a mistake or a poorly phrased sentence you missed while reading it in your head.

16. Have you or your designer created any custom graphics for the offer, including any needed ads for affiliates or partners?

MONEY MATTERS

17. Set a clear monetary goal for the launch. How many sales do you want to see, and how much net income? (In other words, what will success look like?)

18. Advise the merchant account or bank of incoming funds.*

19. Create a backup plan for incoming funds if necessary (get an additional merchant account, plan to switch all payments to PayPal, etc.).

20. Can you add another payment option for anyone who has trouble placing an order?

21. For a high-priced product, can you offer a payment plan? (Note: It's common to offer a slight discount for customers paying in full. This serves as an incentive for customers who prefer to pay all at once while providing an alternative for those who need to pay over time.)

THE NIGHT BEFORE

22. Clear as much email as possible in addition to any other online tasks so you can focus on the big day tomorrow.

23. Write a strong launch message to your lists of readers, customers, and/or affiliates.

24. Prepare a blog post and any needed social media posts (if applicable).

25. Set two alarm clocks to ensure that you're wide awake and available at least one hour before the scheduled launch.

THE BIG MORNING

26. Schedule your launch time to suit your audience, not you. All things being equal, it's usually best to launch early in the morning, East Coast time.

*Merchant accounts are paranoid about large sums of money arriving in a short period of time. If you don't give them a heads-up, you might run into problems.

27. Soft launch at least ten minutes early to make sure everything is working. It's better for you to find the problems than to have your customers find them!

28. Write the first three to five buyers to say thanks and ask, "Did everything go OK in the order process?" (Side benefit: These buyers are probably your biggest fans anyway, so they'll appreciate the personal check-in.)

29. As long as it's possible, send a quick personal note to every buyer in addition to the automated thank-you that goes out. (If it's not possible every time, do it as often as you can.)

PROMOTION (CAN BE DONE ON THE DAY OF LAUNCH OR BEFORE)

30. *Most important:* Ask for help spreading the word. Many readers, prospects, and acquaintances will help by telling their friends and followers, but you have to ask them.

31. Write to affiliates with a reminder about the new offering.

32. Write to journalists or media contacts, if appropriate.

33. Post on Twitter, Facebook, LinkedIn, and any other social networks you already participate in. (It's not usually a good idea to join a new network just to promote something.)

FOLLOW-UP (DO THIS IN ADVANCE)

34. Write the general thank-you message that all buyers will receive when purchasing.

35. If applicable, write the first message for your email follow-up series that buyers will receive.

36. Outline additional content for future communication and plan to schedule it after you recover from the launch.

GOING ABOVE AND BEYOND

37. How can you overdeliver and surprise your customers with this

product? Can you include additional deliverables or some kind of unadvertised benefit?

38. Is there anything special you can do to thank your customers? (For a high-price launch, send postcards to each buyer; for something extra, call a few of your customers on the phone.)

THE SECOND TO LAST STEP

39. Don't forget to celebrate. It's a big day that you've worked up to for a long time. Go out to your favorite restaurant, have a glass of wine, buy something you've had your eye on for a while, or otherwise do something as a personal reward. You've earned it.

THE VERY LAST STEP

40. Start thinking about the next launch. What can you build on from this one? What did you learn that can help you create something even better next time?

Remember, many customers will support you for life as long as you keep providing them with great value. It's much easier to sell to an existing customer than to a new one, so work hard to overdeliver and plan ahead for the next project. (For example, when promising a thirty-nine-step checklist, throw in an extra step.)

Post-Launch: It's Not Over

After the launch, you may be tempted to take a break, and you probably should do something to celebrate or rest. But make it a short break, because what happens next is important. During the launch process, a lot of people were paying attention to you. You've captured additional attention and trust in the form of new customers. Other prospects who considered the offer didn't find it compelling at this time, but perhaps you can serve them with something else later.

Always return to the all-important value question: How can you help people more? After their big launch, Adam and Karol went back to their own businesses and active lives. Adam used part of his proceeds to buy an RV and tour the country with his family, and Karol began an unconventional pilgrimage to visit every roller coaster in America.

At the same time, they kept thinking ahead, planning another big project that would result in more sales, more customers, and more impact.

KEY POINTS

- A good launch is like a Hollywood movie: You first hear about it far in advance, then you hear more about it before the debut, then you watch as crowds of people anxiously queue up for the opening.

- A good launch blends strategy with tactics. *Strategy* refers to "why" questions such as story, offer, and long-term plan. *Tactics* refers to "how" questions such as timing, price, and specific pitch.

- A series of regular communications with prospects before the launch will help you re-create the Hollywood experience with an audience of any size.

- Tell a good story and be sure to consider the question of timeliness: Why should people care about your offer *now*?

- Use the Thirty-Nine-Step Product Launch Checklist as a model. Not every step may apply to you, and you may want to add steps of your own.

ADVERTISING IS LIKE SEX: ONLY LOSERS PAY FOR IT.

"Good things happen to those who hustle."

—ANAÏS NIN

One hundred and twenty miles from Boston in rural New Hampshire, hundreds of artists and art lovers gather twice a year for a communal experience. Before coming to the area, many of them connect online, arranging car-share services and planning meetups. After settling into lakeside cottages, they learn from professionals and spend time with one another, old friends and new friends alike.

It all started five years ago when Elizabeth MacCrellish was feeling isolated from other artists and wanted to create more of a sense of community in her rural area. "I invited my friends to join me for a weekend gathering centered on the arts," she explained. She planned for a few dozen people, but 135 showed up—mostly from the West Coast, far from the small New England group she had expected.

Thus was born Squam Art Workshops, named after a lake in central New Hampshire. After that initial gathering, Elizabeth repeated the experience, first on an annual basis and then twice a year. The audience is one-third professional artists and two-thirds "regular people" with day jobs who enjoy arts and crafts as a hobby. Hundreds of people now come to each sold-out gathering.

As the workshops grew, Elizabeth pulled back to regroup. She did no traditional advertising of any kind, but more people kept signing up, strictly through word of mouth. In the third year of Squam, Elizabeth added an extra session in a new location . . . and ended up regretting it. She was tired and decided to spend the next year "dialing back and taking stock." (She was initially reluctant about speaking to me for this book, but warmed up after I promised to write about the importance of community and relationships in her work.)

To register for Squam, attendees have to mail in their payment and information. This old-school system is one way that Elizabeth maintains a close connection with her tribe. She also carefully assigns people to specific cottages to ensure that newcomers are welcomed and plays Whack-A-Mole in delicately preventing cliques from forming. Invitations to take the Squam show on the road have arrived from the United Kingdom, Australia, and a dozen cities in North America; she always declines.

"I'm not a businessperson," she says. "I just do what feels right, and it keeps getting more interesting." Elizabeth isn't against capitalism, but she wants to be sure that the growth of her business happens in a way that is comfortable for her. Midway through one of our phone calls, she likened her business model to the Amish, talking about a time when she visited a New England farmer's market. Self-reliance is a core value in most Amish communities, and nearly everyone participates in commerce one way or another. But there is very little actual salesmanship; the molasses cookies and apple strudel sell themselves. Even for high-ticket items, prices are nonnegotiable—take it or leave it.

Elizabeth began the workshops as a personal project that grew into a sustainable business. "I never set out to build something more than a structured encounter with friends," she says. Five years later, managing Squam—and making sure it grows in the right way—is Elizabeth's full-time work. After the initial success, at least eight different workshops offering similar retreats sprang up elsewhere, many of which were founded by previous attendees who sought to replicate the event in their own way. It didn't matter, though—the original Squam was the experience you just had to have for yourself.

What Is Hustling?

This chapter is all about *hustling,* or how to get the word out about a project. What does hustling mean? There are a few ways to look at it, but I like the approach in this poster by Joey Roth:

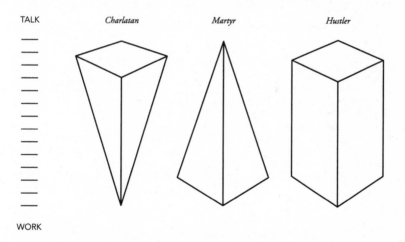

The distinction between the three icons represents the difference (and the likely success or lack of success) of a person or business hoping to promote something for sale. A *charlatan* is all talk, with nothing to back up their claims. A *martyr* is all action with plenty of good work to talk about, but remains unable or unwilling to do the talking. A *hustler* represents the ideal combination: work and talk fused together.

Being willing to promote in an authentic, non-sleazy manner is a core attribute of microbusiness success. As Elizabeth's story illustrates, sometimes the best hustling lies in creating a great offer and getting people to talk about it. In other cases, you want to have as many of the right kind of customers as possible, so there's nothing wrong with putting yourself forward.

In my work, the hustler image on the right is pretty much what I try to do every day as a writer and entrepreneur: lots of creating and lots of connecting. The connecting (i.e., the talk) isn't always directly related to the work at hand—sometimes I'm supporting other people with their hustling—but on a good day, there's plenty of creating and plenty of connecting.

Another way to look at it is

Style without substance = flash

(Also, no one respects these people.)

Substance without style = unknown

(Everyone who knows these people respects them, but not many people know them.)

Style with substance = impact

(This is the goal.)

When you're first getting started with a project, how do you go from martyr to hustler? It's simple. First things first: Take the time to make something worth talking about—don't be a charlatan. But then start with everyone you know and ask for their help. Make a list of at least fifty people and divide them into categories (colleagues from a former job, college friends, acquaintances, etc.). As soon as the project is good to go, at least in beta form, touch base by sending them a quick note. Here's a sample message:

Hi [name],

I wanted to quickly let you know about a new project I'm working on.

It's called [name of business or project], and the goal is to [main benefit]. We hope to [big goal, improvement, or idea].

Don't worry, I haven't added you to any lists and I won't be spamming you, but if you like the idea and would like to help out, here's what you can do:

[Action Point 1]
[Action Point 2]

Thanks again for your time.

Note that you're not sending mass messages or sharing anyone's private info with the world; each message is personal, although the content is largely the same. You're also not "selling" anyone on the project; you're just letting people know what you're up to and *inviting* them to participate further if they'd like to. The action points can vary, but they should probably relate to joining a contact list (this way you have their permission to touch base with them further) and letting other people know about the project.

The next step is to incorporate hustling into your ongoing regular work.

If You Build It, They Might Come . . .

It might happen by magic, but you'll probably have to tell them about it. Even with Elizabeth MacCrellish's low-key Amish selling model, she still began her summer workshops by recruiting friends and supporters. This is where hustling comes in. If half the work is building the house and the other half is selling it, here's how a few other people sold it:

We spent no money on advertising for the first five months we were open. Instead, we decided to allocate more than half of our opening costs to have a thirty-by-fifty-foot mural of a bright and colorful tree painted on the side of the stand-alone brick building we're in. That speaks way louder than any ad we could ever place. —Karen Starr, Hazel Tree Interiors

When I launched my membership program, I decided to start with some beta testers. I invited a hundred of my top prospects to try it out for the first two months before I opened membership . . . but I didn't send them an email invite. Instead, I sent a hostage letter in a brown paper bag—folded and taped. People really got a kick out of it, and it worked! The letter led to a sales page with a personal video invite from me. —Alyson Stanfield, Art Biz Coach

We initially imagined a community of thousands for our triathlon and Ironman distance training programs. In reality, fewer members meant deeper roots and a much more powerful experience for everyone. Unlike most programs, which try to keep pushing the price higher, we reward our members by *decreasing* the price the longer they remain in the program. This is because we recognize that the more experience they have, the more they can help other members . . . and the more active they are in recruiting new members to join as well. —Patrick McCrann, Endurance Nation

---

First Things First: What Do You Have to Say?

I was sitting in a large conference room with my friend Jonathan Fields (also mentioned in Chapter 7). Jonathan is an ex-lawyer turned serial entrepreneur and author. Several presenters were having a group discussion on building a tribe of followers, and someone in the room asked a question about writing a book: "What's the first step?"

One of the speakers gave a list of four or five ideas, and then at the end he said, "Oh, when you plan to write a book, you should also think about what you have to say."

Jonathan and I looked at each other with the same thought: "Uh, isn't that the *first* step?"

Getting the message out about your business is like writing a book: Before you do anything else, think about what you have to say. What's the message? Why is it important now, and why will people want to know about it?

The Strategic Giving Marketing Plan

Freely give, freely receive: It works. The more you focus your business on providing a valuable service and helping people, the more your business will grow. A number of the subjects of our case studies discussed how giving (often described in different ways but with the same meaning) has been a core value of their business. One of the best descriptions came from Megan Hunt, the Omaha dressmaker we met in Chapters 1 and 3:

My marketing plan could be called strategic giving. When I launch a new line of dresses each year, I contact two or three influential bloggers and create a custom dress for them, which always brings in tons of new customers when they write about it. But most importantly, I turn my attention toward my clients. Often, I upgrade someone's shipping to overnight for free, or double someone's order, or include a copy of my favorite book with a handwritten note. I like to package my products for shipping like a gift to my best friend. This strategy has been a huge contributor to fast growth and popularity in my industry.

John Morefield, an unemployed architect during a time when jobs were scarce, set up shop in a Seattle farmer's market with a sign that read "5-Cent Architecture Advice." In exchange for a nickel, he would give advice on any problem that homeowners, real estate agents, or anyone else brought to him. The 5-cent advice was effectively a lead-generation program that might lead to additional business, but John legitimately and genuinely offered professional advice without the expectation of more than a nickel.

As news spread of the 5-cent architect, John got free advertising from CNN, NPR, the BBC, and numerous other media outlets. Because of the attention—and new clients who came in through the farmer's market—John is now a successful *self-employed* architect, a key distinction from his peers who are still trying to get hired at firms.

Another way to practice strategic giving is to deliberately *not* take advantage of every opportunity to increase income. As my own business grew and I received more public attention, I began to receive a lot of requests for consulting sessions. I never really saw myself as a consultant, but I figured, Why not? If this is what people want, maybe I can do it. I created a page on my website, received plenty of interest, and conducted a few sessions as a test. Long story short, the whole thing felt false and inauthentic to me. I had helped lots of people with specific problems before, but not on a pay-per-time basis. When I talked with people who had paid for access to me, I felt physically ill. I realized my discomfort was in doing it for money, so I stopped.

I still do some limited consulting whenever I can, but now I do it for free. With the right people and on my own terms, I enjoy it—especially without the pressure of knowing they are paying me to deliver. I'm not always able to offer helpful advice, but I know that when I can be helpful, that person will likely be there for me at some point in the future. It's not about keeping score or trading favors on a quid pro quo basis; it's about genuinely caring and trying to improve someone else's life whenever you can.*

Like any kind of marketing, this practice can be manipulated or abused. Tourists landing at the international terminal at LAX are met outside by friendly people with official-looking clipboards who offer to help with directions to the city. "Hey, where are you headed today?" they ask. "Can I be of assistance?" After they provide directions or answer questions from unsuspecting tourists, there's a pitch: "I'm working today on behalf of a great organization. Can you help us out with a donation?" The implied message is, *I just helped you . . . now it's your turn.*

This isn't the kind of strategic giving that serves your interests well in the long term. The intention of the airport solicitors isn't to be helpful; they are merely using helpfulness as a tool to gain the trust of unsuspecting tourists. Strategic giving is about being genuinely, *truly* helpful without the thought of a potential payback.

*I use this example to illustrate that having a good opportunity doesn't mean you should pursue it. I'm not opposed to consulting in general. It just wasn't a good fit for me.

Building Relationships Is a Strategy, Not a Tactic

Getting to know people, helping them, and asking for help yourself can take you far. This is not a non-profit endeavor; it often pays off in real money (with interest!) over time. But it is a long-term strategy, not a short-term tactic to copy for quick success.

Originally from South Dakota, Scott Meyer was working as a professor of peace studies in the Arctic Circle in Tromsø, Norway. (It was a long way from home, but the winters were familiar, he explains.) Meanwhile, his brother John was a consultant for Accenture in Minneapolis. Scott and John's migration away from their roots was normal—back in South Dakota, there was a clear divide between "people who stayed" and "people who got out."

After a few years away, both Scott and John began to think of returning home with a mission. South Dakota wasn't a bad place, and there was a growing community of entrepreneurs there, many of whom had a problem. Small businesses in the region tended to be run by people with fewer technical skills than those in Minneapolis or Chicago, the region's main hubs. "Around here," Scott told me, "people tend to use an old-school phone book to contact someone, and many business owners struggle with using email effectively. We knew we could help them grow their business."

Scott and John founded 9 Clouds, a consultancy designed to help local businesses reach more customers through improved communication while gently educating them along the way. They give clients the fish by helping them reach new customers. Their clients are smart but worry about wasting time with new technology. 9 Clouds shows them the benefits of learning new tools that have been proved to be useful.

The firm works hard to drum up business, but it focuses first on drumming up value. "Every chance we get, we talk and share information with others and support them in their work," Scott says. "It may not be a sale or partnership, but building those relationships today always comes back around for new opportunities tomorrow." The community is noticing: 9 Clouds won second place in the South Dakota Governor's Giant Vision contest, and John was recognized by *BusinessWeek* as an up-and-coming leader. 9 Clouds did $45,000 in net income during the first six months of operation, $180,000 the next year, and is now on track to becoming a mid-six-figure business.

First Say Yes, Then Say "Hell Yeah"

Other business books will tell you about saying no: how you should guard your time, "only do what you're good at," and turn down far more requests than you accept. As a business grows over time and options for growth become more selective, that may indeed be useful advice.

But what if you took the opposite approach, especially at first? What if you deliberately said yes to every request unless you had a good reason not to? The next time someone asks for something, try saying yes and see what it leads to. Whatever success I've had in my own work thus far has always come from saying yes, not from saying no.

Derek Sivers, who founded a business he later sold for $22 million (he then donated the money to a charitable trust), offers an alternative strategy: As things get busy, evaluate your options according to the "hell yeah" test. When you're presented with an opportunity, don't just think about its merits or how busy you are. Instead, think about how it makes you feel. If you feel only so-so about it, turn it down and move on. But if the opportunity would be exciting and meaningful—so much so that you can say "hell yeah" when you think about it—find a way to say yes.

Give Something Away and Watch People Jump

Are the crickets chirping in your business? There's nothing like a contest or giveaway to get people engaged. I regularly receive 1,000 comments or more on a single Facebook post giving away a $15 book. I used to wonder, "What is the last person thinking? 'Nine hundred ninety-nine people have entered, but maybe I'll be the lucky one'?" Over time I realized that it wasn't so much about winning as it was about social participation. If all your friends are putting their names down, why wouldn't you do the same thing?*

The difference between a contest and a giveaway is fairly simple: A *contest* involves some kind of competition or judging, whereas a *giveaway* is a straight-up free offer provided to winners through random entries. There are pros and cons to each: A contest usually requires more work for both the aspiring winners and the business hosting the contest, but it can generate more interest. A giveaway is quick and easy and can generate a large quantity of entries, but since there's usually nothing to do other than put your name down, the typical giveaway doesn't create much real engagement. For the best results, experiment over time with both methods.

The $10,000, Ten-Hour Marketing and Sex Experiment

"In the future, marketing will be like sex: Only the losers pay for it."

This widely circulated statement first appeared in a December 2010 article in *Fast Company* magazine. Guess what? The future is here. It may not be completely for losers, but the role of paid advertising in marketing has long since changed. The vast majority of case-study

---

*I thought 1,000 entries for a basic giveaway was pretty good until Jaden Hair from *Steamy Kitchen* told me she receives as many as 50,000 entries for her giveaways, all for a prize as simple as a set of cookbooks.

The One-Page Promotion Plan

Goal: To actively and effectively recruit new prospects to your business without getting overwhelmed.

DAILY

· Maintain a regular social media presence without getting sidetracked or overwhelmed. Post one to three helpful items, respond to questions, and touch base with anyone who needs help.

· Monitor one or two key metrics (no more!). Read more about this in Chapter 13.

WEEKLY

· Ask for help or joint promotions from colleagues and make sure you are being helpful to them as well.

· Maintain regular communication with prospects and customers.

AT LEAST MONTHLY

· Connect with existing customers to make sure they are happy. (Ask: "Is there anything else I can do for you?")

· Prepare for an upcoming event, contest, or product launch (see Chapter 8).

ONCE IN A WHILE

· Perform your own business audit (see Chapter 12) to find missing opportunities that can be turned into active projects.

· Ensure that you are regularly working toward building something significant, not just reacting to things as they appear.

subjects I talked with built their customer base without any paid advertising at all; they did so largely through word of mouth.

While thinking about the quote and drafting this chapter, I decided to conduct an unscientific experiment to measure paid ads versus free hustling. Over the course of a month, I spent $10,000 on carefully selected ads and sponsorship for my Travel Hacking Cartel service. I also spent ten hours hustling, writing guest posts, recruiting a joint venture with another service, touching base with journalist contacts, and so on. Here are the results:

Ad Cost: $10,000 (+2 hours of setup)	vs.	Hustling Cost: 10 Hours Zero Dollars
Number of New Customers: 78		Number of New Customers: 84
Estimated Value of New Customers: $7020		Estimated Value of New Customers: $7560

Approximate hour-per-hustle value: **$756**

Do we have a clear winner? I think so, but with a couple of disclaimers. First, one could say that I had access to relationships that others don't have and those relationships were what determined the high hour-per-hustle value. This may be partly true. However, the whole point of hustling is to put your relationships to good use, whatever they are. Not everyone may be able to earn $756 per hustling hour. However, some situations could have produced an even higher hustling value.

It is also true that hustling time is not unlimited. If I had $100,000 to spend instead of $10,000, the situation might indeed be different. Combining hustling with paid advertising (again, carefully selected) could be a viable option for some. The point is that hustling can take you far. When you're thinking about how to get the word out and build your business, think about hustling first and paid advertising later (if at all).

• • •

One objection to the hustling and relationship-building strategies described in this chapter is that they take time. Well, of course they do—they're a big part of your work. But if you're worried about spending all day on a social networking site, you can avoid doing that by sticking to a series of quick check-ins. I maintain a text file of information and links to share, and a couple of times a day I go online and post something. At the same time, I scan all the messages that have come through for me and respond to as many as possible. Although I sometimes spend more time out of habit or interest, the whole process doesn't have to take any longer than ten to fifteen minutes a day.

The point is to do what makes sense to you. Get up in the morning and get to work. Make something worth talking about and then talk about it. Who do you know? How can they help? And of course, the answer lies in being incredibly helpful yourself.

KEY POINTS

- If you're not sure where to spend your business development time, spend 50 percent on creating and 50 percent on connecting. The most powerful channel for getting the word out usually starts with people you already know.

- If you build it, they might come . . . but you'll probably need to let them know what you've built and how to get there.

- When you're first getting started, say yes to every reasonable request. Become more selective (consider the "hell yeah" test) as you become more established.

- Use the One-Page Promotion Plan to maintain a regular schedule of connecting with people as you also spend time building other parts of your business.

> **"Money is better than poverty,
> if only for financial reasons."**
> —WOODY ALLEN

Naomi Dunford was a teenage mother and a high-school drop-out. By the time she was pregnant with her second child, she was living in a homeless shelter. After making it out of the shelter by working odd jobs, Naomi was determined to improve her circumstances however she could. Despite the obvious disadvantages—being a mom at age seventeen, leaving high school—she also had a few things going for her. Her dad had built several businesses from scratch, imparting knowledge and experience along the way. Her mom was a marketer. And back in the day, her grandfather was in advertising. In other words, marketing was in Naomi's blood, so it wasn't a huge stretch for her to imagine herself in a different life.

Without sharing her background with potential customers at first, Naomi opened a consulting company called IttyBiz. Tag line: "Marketing for businesses without marketing departments." Later she would add products, courses, and referrals to other professionals, but Naomi started with a single consulting service: the service of brainstorming. Over the course of an hour and for an initial fee of $250, she would evaluate marketing ideas and provide feedback on ways to improve them. Nothing more, nothing less.

You might wonder how many people pay for this service (answer: a lot), and whether it's worth it (answer: keep reading). Naomi is originally from London, Ontario, but I met her in London, England, where she was living near her mother. While riding the tube around the city and wandering through an outdoor clothing market, I asked for her advice on a situation in my business. She listened for two minutes and asked a few clarifying questions. Then, without much of a pause, she said, "Here's what you should do," and gave me a list of specific actions and ideas while I frantically wrote them down. I took her advice and spent a few hours applying it in my next project. As a result, I made at least $15,000 more over the next year because of her action list. (I didn't pay Naomi's fee of $250, but I hope she appreciates this extended testimonial.)

As she sharpened her message and connected with more people, the business grew. At the end of her first full year, Naomi published a short video explaining how she had earned almost $200,000 so far. This came as a big surprise to the online world, because Naomi wasn't known very well—she wasn't an Internet celebrity, she didn't have a million followers—and in fact, a lot of people who stumbled upon her website were immediately turned off by the coarse language and her distinct "call it like I see it" style. Article titles included "What to Do When You're Scared Shitless" and "Moral of the Story: Topless Edition (with Photos)." But Naomi's audience wasn't put off at all.

One of the things Naomi does well is continuously remind her clients about the need for actually making money. This may sound simple, but busy entrepreneurs can easily become overwhelmed with all kinds of projects and tasks that have nothing to do with making money. Putting the focus on income and cash flow—measuring everything else against those standards—ensures that a business remains healthy. Here's how Naomi explains it:

> Remember that the goal of business is profit. It's not being liked, or having a huge social media presence, or having amazing products that nobody buys. It is not having a beautiful website, or perfectly crafted email newsletters, or an incredibly popular blog. In larger businesses, this is called accountability to shareholders. Business is not a popularity contest. The CEO doesn't get away with saying, "But look at all these people who like us on Facebook!" Shareholders will not accept that. You are the majority shareholder in your business, and you have to protect your investment. You have to make sure that your recurring activities are as directly tied to making money as possible. There's nothing wrong with having a hobby, but if you want to call it a business, you have to make money.

Naomi is right: On any given day, there are all kinds of things you can do that have nothing to do with making money—but you should be careful about those distractions, because without the money, there is no business. Many aspiring business owners make two common, related mistakes: thinking too much about where to get money to start their project and thinking too little about where the business income will come from. Fixing these problems (or avoiding them in the first place) requires a simple solution: Spend as little money as possible and make as much money as you can.

Part I: Hang On to Your Wallet

Inspired by her second child, Heather Allard invented two wearable baby blankets that became a worldwide sensation. The blankets were featured on *Access Hollywood* and sold in more than 200 stores, and it was all she could do to keep up. After the birth of her third child in 2006, Heather sold the products to a larger company in order to spend more time with the family. Success! She wasn't done with entrepreneurship, though; the next step was to help other women, especially mothers, learn to do what she had accomplished. She started her next business, The Mogul Mom, with the goal of mentoring busy women who wanted to create more independence through a small business. The baby blanket business was highly successful, but it also became a high-spending operation as the product took off. On reflection, Heather realized that she would need to run her second act differently:

> I had gotten into a *ton* of start-up debt with my product company and spent thousands on things that I absolutely did *not* need (big advertising campaigns, a custom e-commerce website, a publicist, etc.), and I definitely did not want to do that with The Mogul Mom. Therefore, when I spend money on The Mogul Mom, it's for things that will continue to build my brand and boost my sales while allowing me ample time with my family—things like Web design, payments to a small group of contributors, or a new computer.

The distinction Heather points out at the end is important: She's not reluctant to spend money on things that will (1) build her brand and (2) boost her sales. This kind of spending can grow a business. If you can spend $100 and create $200 in value from it, why wouldn't you? It's the other kind of spending—the unproven ad campaigns and unneeded custom websites—that Heather learned to stay away from. Lesson: Spend only on things that have a direct relationship to sales.

The stories from Naomi and Heather illustrate two important principles, both related to money. The first principle is that a business should always focus on profit. (Always remember, no money, no business.) The second principle is that borrowing money or investing a lot of money to start a business is completely optional.

This doesn't mean that there are no examples of businesses that have done well through traditional methods; it just means that *borrowing is no longer essential*. Don't think of it as a necessary evil; think of it as an undesirable option to be pursued only if you have a way to limit risk or are sure you know what you're doing.

If you don't know what you're doing when you're starting out, that's OK, you're in good company. Almost every entrepreneur pursues projects with a much-trial-and-much-error system. But since it's easy to try things without losing your shirt, why seek investment and go into debt for something that may or may not work?

It's completely possible to start on a very low budget without hindering the odds of success. Consider the reports of many in our study group:

- Chelly Vitry started a business as a tour guide for Denver food lovers, connecting them to restaurants and food producers. Startup costs: $28. Recent annual income: $60,000.

- Michael Trainer started a media production company for $2,500, the cost of a nice camera, which he later sold to recoup the cost in full. He then went on to work with two Nobel Prize winners: the Acumen fund and the Carter Center.

- Tara Gentile started her small publishing business for $80, hoping to earn enough money to be able to stay home with her daughter. One year later, she earned enough money ($75,000) that her husband could stay home as well.

- Chris Dunphy and Cherie Ve Ard started Technomadia, a software consultancy for health-care providers, for $125. The business now produces net income of more than $75,000 as Chris and Cherie travel the world.

- A former store designer for Starbucks, Charlie Pabst needed a $3,500 computer for his Seattle design business. But after he had the powerful machine and a $100 business license, he was good to go. Annual income: just under $100,000.

These stories are not outliers. When I began the research for this book, I received more than 1,500 nominations, with similar stories from all over the world. You can see the range of startup costs from our study group in the graph below. The average cost of the initial investment was $610.60.*

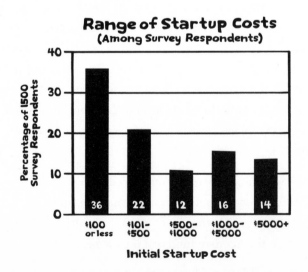

Range of Startup Costs
(Among Survey Respondents)

Percentage of 1500 Survey Respondents

36	22	12	16	14
$100 or less	$101–$500	$500–$1000	$1000–$5000	$5000+

Initial Startup Cost

*The median cost was $125. If we discount the 15 percent of outliers at the upper and lower ranges, the average startup cost was $408 and the median cost remained $125.

You might expect that certain types of businesses are easier to start with limited funds, and that is correct. It's also the whole point: Since it's so much easier to start a microbusiness, why do something different unless or until you know what you're doing? Small is beautiful, and all things considered, small is often better.

Unconventional Fundraising from Kickstarter to Car Loans

What if you've thought it through and you do need to raise money somehow? Whenever possible, the best option is your own savings. You'll be highly invested in the success of the project, and you won't be in debt to anyone else. But if this isn't possible, you can also consider "crowdraising" funds for your project through a service such as Kickstarter.com. Shannon Okey did this with a project to boost her craft publishing business. She asked for $5,000 and received $12,480 in twenty days thanks to a nice video and well-written copy.

Before going to the masses, Shannon went to her bank for a small loan. Her business was profitable and promising, with several new publications coming out over the next year. This wasn't just any bank. It was a community bank in Ohio where she had an excellent personal and business relationship. Shannon was a meticulous bookkeeper with a conservative attitude toward finances; she brought along detailed sales figures and a clear plan to repay the money. Unfortunately, when she mentioned "craft publishing," she was dead in the water. "They looked at me like I was a silly, silly woman who couldn't possibly know anything about running a business," she said.

The rejection turned into an opportunity. Taking the project on Kickstarter generated both funds *and* widespread interest in the project. Nearly three hundred backers came through with donations ranging from $10 to $500, leaving the project fully funded with capital to spare. Oh, and Shannon was not one for going quietly.

After she reached the $10,000 level in her Kickstarter campaign, she printed out the front page of the site, wrapped the page around a lollipop, and sent it off to the bank's underwriters. "I think they got the message," she says.

As I collected stories for the book, I was mostly interested in people who avoided debt completely. But I did hear two fun stories about borrowing money that I thought were worth sharing. On a flight from Hong Kong to London, Emma Reynolds and her future business partner Bruce Morton had an idea for a consultancy that would work with big companies to improve their staffing and resourcing. They calculated that they would need at least $17,000 to start the new firm. There was just one problem . . . or actually, two: Emma was twenty-three and unlikely to get a business loan, and Bruce was going through a divorce and would also be a poor candidate for a business loan. Somewhere during the twelve-hour flight, one of them realized that although they couldn't get a business loan, they could probably get a car loan.

Bruce proceeded to do just that, borrowing $17,000 for a car and then investing the funds in the business with Emma instead. They paid back the car loan within ten months, and the bank never found out that there was no actual car. Now the firm employs twenty people, is highly profitable, and has multiple offices in four countries.*

Finally, here's a fun story from Kristin McNamara, who started a California gym specializing in climbing:

To fund the latest incarnation of the gym, we called upon the community to "invest" in us, much like a three-year CD. We

---

* Even though it worked out OK for Emma and Bruce, borrowing money for a nonexistent car and using the funds for a business was a bold move. As they say on TV, you might not want to try this at home.

offered 3 percent above prime, which is more than you could get then or now, and people I've never even seen at the facility came up with the cash to get it started. My partner and I, the founders, are the only paid full-time staff, and we just hired someone to manage the volunteers for us for a small stipend. Our community fundraising project brought in $80,000.

As these lessons in improvisation show, if you need to raise money, there's more than one way to do it.

Part II: Make More Money (Three Key Principles to Focus on Profit)

As we've seen, it's usually much more important to focus your efforts on making money as soon as possible than on borrowing startup capital. In different ways, many of our case studies focused on three key principles that helped them become profitable (either profitable in the first place or more profitable as the business grew). I've noticed that the same thing holds true in my businesses. The more I focus on these things, the better off I am. In short, they are as follows:

1. Price your product or service in relation to the benefit it provides, not the cost of producing it.
2. Offer customers a limited range of prices.
3. Get paid more than once for the same thing.

We'll look at each of them below.

Principle 1: Base Prices on Benefits, Not Costs

In Chapter 2, we looked at benefits versus features. Remember that a feature is descriptive ("These clothes fit well and look nice") and a benefit is the value someone receives from the item in question ("These clothes make you feel healthy and attractive"). We tend to default to talking about features, but since most purchases are emotional decisions, it's much more persuasive to talk about benefits.

Just as you should usually place more emphasis on the benefits of your offering than on the features, you should think about basing the price of your offer on the benefit—not the actual cost or the amount of time it takes to create, manufacture, or fulfill what you are selling. In fact, the *wrong* way to decide on pricing is to think about how much time it took to make it or how much your time is "worth." How much your time is worth is a completely subjective matter. Bill Clinton makes as much as $200,000 for a single one-hour speech. You might not want to pay Clinton (or any president) $200,000 to speak at your next family pizza night, but for whatever reason, some companies are willing to invest that much.

When you base your pricing on the benefits you provide, be prepared to stand your ground, because some people will always complain about the price being too high no matter what it is. Almost none of the people I met with talked about thriving in their new businesses because they always offered the lowest price. What works for Walmart probably won't work for you or me. Very few businesses will succeed on the basis of such a cutthroat strategy; that's why competing on value is so much better.*

Gary Leff, the frequent flyer guy who helps busy people book their vacations, charges a flat rate for the service ($250 at press time). Sometimes it takes him a fair amount of work to research and book the trip, but other times he gets lucky and it can take as little as two minutes of research and a ten-minute phone call. Gary

---

*Once in a while someone will complain that something I sell is "too expensive." I always reply that it may indeed be too expensive for them and I'd never try to convince them otherwise, but only the market will decide if it's too expensive for other people.

knows that the people he's booking the trip for don't care whether it takes ten minutes or two hours; they are paying for his expertise in getting the flights they want.

> Time cost: variable, but averages thirty minutes per booking
> Benefit: first-class and business-class tickets for worldwide vacations
> Cost: $250 (key point: does not vary based on time)

Tsilli Pines, who makes contemporary Judaic stationery, created a Haggadah (a booklet used at the Passover meal) that most frequently is sold in bulk. Single copies are available, but far more people choose a bundle of five or ten.

> Materials cost: $3 each
> Benefit: nicely designed memento for families to use when observing Passover
> Cost to buyers: $14 each (key point: not directly related to the materials cost)

We could trace this theme throughout almost every story in the book. Some examples are even more extreme, especially in information publishing. Every day, people purchase $1,000+ courses that cost virtually nothing to distribute; all the costs are in development and initial marketing. When you think about the price of a new project, ask yourself: "How will this idea improve my customers' lives, and what is that improvement worth to them?" Then set your price accordingly, while still being clear that the offer is a great value.

Principle 2: Offer a (Limited) Range of Prices

Choosing an initial price for your service that is based on the benefit provided to customers is the most important principle to ensure profitability. But to create *optimum* profitability or at least to build more cushion into your business model, you'll next want to present more than one price for your offer. This practice typically makes a huge difference to the bottom line, because it allows you to increase income without increasing your customer base.

Look at Apple, which famously produces very few products and doesn't bother to compete on price. Even though there are few products, there is always a range of prices and options. You can buy the latest iGadget or computer at the entry level (which, knowing Apple, isn't cheap), one or more midlevels, or one "superuser" high-end level. The leadership team at Apple—and anyone using a similar model—knows that this kind of pricing allows the company to earn much more money than it otherwise would. This is the case partly because some people will always choose the biggest and best, even if the biggest and best is much more expensive than the regular version. These kinds of sales will increase the overall selling price.

Also, having a high-end version creates an "anchor price." When we see a superhigh price, we tend to consider the lower price as much more reasonable . . . thus creating a fair bargain in our minds. The internal thinking goes like this: "Wow, $2 million for the latest MacBook is a lot, but hey, the $240,000 model is almost as good."

Let's look at an example of two pricing options: one offered at a set price and one on a tiered structure. Keep in mind that you can substitute any prices here to apply this to another business.

Option 1: The World's Greatest Widget
Price: $87

Option 1 is simple and presents the choice as follows: Do you want to buy this widget or not?

Here's an alternative that is almost always better:

> *Option 2: The World's Greatest Widget*
> Choose Your Preferred Widget Option Below
> 1. Greatest Widget Ever, Budget Version. Price: $87
> 2. Greatest Widget Ever, Even Better Version. Price: $129
> 3. Greatest Widget Ever, Exclusive Premium Version. Price: $199

Option 2 presents the choice as follows: Which widget package would you like to buy?

Chances are, some consumers will choose the Exclusive Premium Version, others will choose the Budget Version, but most will opt for the Even Better Version. You don't want to go too crazy, but you can experiment with this model to add yet another tier in the form of a "*really* premium version" at the top or a "freemium" version at the bottom that lets customers try part of the service without paying anything.

Now let's look at how the money works out for both of these options.

Option 1:	*Option 2:*
20 sales @ $87	20 sales @ variable prices
	(14 choose middle,
	3 choose budget,
	3 choose premium)
Total income: $1,740	Total income: $2,664
Income per sale: $87	Income per sale: $133
Difference: $924 total, or $46 per sale	

The key to this strategy is to offer a *limited* range of prices: not so many as to create confusion but enough to provide buyers with a legitimate choice. Notice the important distinction that naturally happens when you offer a choice: Instead of asking them whether they'd like to buy your widget, you're asking which widget they would like to buy.

Options for creating a price range include: Super-Amazing Version (Gold, First Class, Premium), Product + Setup Help (the same thing sold with special help), and any kind of exclusivity or limited-quantity selection.

You can literally sell the same product at different prices with no other change. As long as you don't imply that there are added features in the higher-price version, it's not unethical. Big companies do it all the time; it's how cell phone carriers, hotels, and airlines make money. To reduce confusion, though, it's better if you can add something with real value to each higher-level version of the offer.

Principle 3: Get Paid More Than Once

The final strategy for making sure your business gets off to a good start is to ensure that your payday doesn't come along only once—you'd much rather have repeated paydays, from the same customers, over and over on a reliable basis. You may have heard of the terms *continuity program, membership site,* and *subscriptions.* They all mean roughly the same thing: getting paid over and over by the same customers, usually for ongoing access to a service or regular delivery of a product.

Back when people read newspapers (actual paper ones), they would subscribe to have them delivered to their doorstep or office. These days, iTunes and Netflix offer subscriptions to your favorite TV show or a regular series of movies. The utility company has a recurring billing program; every month you pay it for the ability to turn the lights on and heat your water. For decades, the Book of the Month Club (in various forms) has delivered new books to its members on a recurring basis.

Almost any business can create a *continuity program*. Speaking of book clubs, there is also a Pickle of the Month Club, an Olive Oil of the Month Club, and a Dog Treat of the Month Club. In Portland, my friend Jessie operates a Cupcake of the Month club. If you like bonsai plants but aren't able to keep them alive very long, the Bonsai of the Month Club is for you, but you'll have to choose among four competing companies that offer different versions.*

Why is getting paid over and over such a big deal? First, because it can bring in a lot of money, and second, because it's reliable income that isn't dependent on external factors. Let's run some quick numbers, assuming you offer a subscription service for $20 a month:

100 subscribers at $20 = monthly revenue of $2,000 *or* yearly revenue of $24,000

1,000 subscribers at $20 = monthly revenue of $20,000 *or* yearly revenue of $240,000

You can tweak either the number of subscribers or the price of the recurring service to see dramatic improvements. For example, adding 50 more subscribers generates $1,000 more per month, or $12,000 more per year. Raising the price to $25 a month with a subscriber base of 1,000 generates $5,000 more per month, or $60,000 more per year. Adjusting *both* options—attracting more subscribers and raising the price—generates an even greater increase.

(Note: Don't get too hung up on the exact numbers here. The point is that in almost every case, a recurring billing model will produce much more income over time than will a single-sale model.)

Even better, after you attract customers to a recurring model

*Yes, these are all real examples. Google them.

(and ensure that you keep them very happy), they are much more likely to purchase other things from you. Brian Clark is an expert at continuity programs, having created a true empire from the art of moving customers from one-time purchases into recurring subscriptions. Here's what he has to say about this process:

> Our general model is to offer a varied line of complementary products and services. Some are one-time purchases that begin the customer's relationship with us, and others are software and hosting services that involve recurring monthly or quarterly billing. While we strive to build all our product lines, the general strategy is to move as many one-time purchase customers as possible to a more lucrative recurring service.
>
> For example, our StudioPress division sells WordPress themes (designs) to online publishers and has over 50,000 customers. These are one-time purchases, although many people end up coming back to purchase additional design options. We also provide ongoing support to all of these customers.
>
> Over time, we offer our Scribe SEO service or our new WordPress hosting service to our StudioPress customers, which transfers the nature of the relationship into one that is much more economically beneficial for us. But the secret ingredient to this migration is the trust we've developed with those customers from the initial one-time purchase. We treat people well, period. This means before an initial sale is made with our free content, and even better once they become a customer, no matter the size of the purchase.
>
> The key to this model is not market share. It's *share of the customer*. And to gain more of each customer's budget, you first have to zealously treat every customer as a "best" customer,

no matter which ones actually end up becoming the proverbial "customer for life."

The most important thing Brian says here is in the last paragraph: "It's not market share; it's share of the customer." Like many of the people in this book, Brian doesn't spend much time worrying about what other people are doing—he worries about improving his customers' lives through helpful services. As a result, he gets paid over and over again.

• • •

Getting paid more than once is great, but be aware of a couple of concerns. First, many consumers are wary of subscriptions, because they worry that they'll keep getting billed for the service after they stop using it or that it will be a big hassle to cancel. (To deal with the second problem, I created a "no pain in the ass" cancellation button for my site.) To encourage broad waves of initial sign-ups, many programs offer free or low-cost trials to get new prospects in the door. This works, but there is often a huge dropout rate after the trial ends. Just be aware of this, and make sure you continue to provide value as long as people are paying.

The $35,000 Experiment

One day I received an intriguing message from one of my customers, who successfully built a new business over the past year and is now making an average of $4,000 to $5,000 a month from his industry. In the email he told me about the results from an interesting experiment. I asked if I could share the results with other customers (and eventually put it in this book), but he was concerned about his competition learning how easy it was to increase profits. He finally said I could share this information as long as I didn't unmask him. Here's his follow-up note to me with the details:

> As mentioned yesterday, I wanted to check something in my product. I set up an experiment that only tested a single variable: price. On one sales page I had $49, and on another $89. Nothing was different at all—same copywriting, same order process, same fulfillment. To be honest, I thought that $49 was a better price, but I had set that price somewhat arbitrarily. Guess what? Conversion went down . . . slightly. But overall income actually increased! This is what really surprised me. I discovered that I could sell less but actually make more money due to the higher price.
>
> I then decided to test it at $99. Why not, right? But from $89 to $99 I saw a bit more of a drop-off, and I got worried. I'm now back at $89, and even with the lower conversion factored in, I worked out that I've given myself a $24 raise on every product that sells. These days we are selling at least four copies a day. If everything else remains consistent, I'll make $35,040 more this year . . . all from one test.
>
> I've decided to do some more tests. :)

Isn't that interesting? Here's how the numbers break down in this example:

FEWER SALES, MORE MONEY

Option 1: $49 price	Option 2: $89 price
2% conversion rate	1.5% conversion rate (a 25% decline)
Sales per 1,000 prospects = 20	Sales per 1,000 prospects =15
Revenue per 1,000 prospects = $980	Revenue per 1,000 prospects = $1,335

Result: five fewer sales, but $355 more revenue

Note that if the conversion rate dropped further, say, to 1 percent instead of 1.5 percent, the price change would not be a good idea. But in some cases, the news is actually better than it is in this example: When you raise the price, you don't always see a drop in the conversion rate. If you successfully raise prices without lowering the conversion rate, it's time to order the champagne.

The point is that experimenting with price is one of the easiest ways to create higher profits (and sustainability) in a business. If you're not sure what price to use for something, try a higher one without changing anything else and see what happens. You might find yourself with an extra $24 per sale—maybe more.

You Have More Than You Think

After I met Naomi Dunford in England, I saw her again a year later in Austin, Texas, where we were both in town for the South by Southwest (SXSW) Interactive Festival. Earlier that day, she had run into a money problem. The problem wasn't a *lack* of money; her business was doing extremely well, on the way to breaking the $1 million a year barrier. The problem was *access* to money. Because Naomi is Canadian but has lived in the United States, the United Kingdom, and elsewhere, she often has issues with her Pay-Pal account being closed as she travels the world, leaving her with plenty of funds in the account but no way to access them. In this case, she needed $900 to register for a conference that had just been announced . . . and would sell out quickly. What to do?

Naomi realized that although she didn't have $900 with her, she probably knew someone in Austin willing to loan her the use of a credit card so she could register. Asking around, she found three volunteers in the first two minutes who all said, "Sure, no problem. Here's my card."

As we talked about it further, we realized that most of us have access to all kinds of financial and social capital that we don't usually think about but could call upon easily if necessary. If one guy hadn't lent her his credit card, someone else would have. The trick was that she had to be willing to think creatively. If she had just said, "Oh, I guess I can't register now," she would have missed out. Being able to think of different means to achieve her goal led Naomi out of the homeless shelter a decade ago and to the highly successful IttyBiz. "Right before starting," she said, "I was taking the bus to work, making 55 percent of a $30,000 income. My phone was cut off from lack of payment. Now I employ six people and help hundreds of others become self-employed."

We all have more than we think. Let's put it to good use.

KEY POINTS

- There's nothing wrong with having a hobby, but if you're operating a business, the primary goal is to make money.

- Going into debt to start a business is completely optional. Every day, people open and operate successful ventures without any kind of outside investment or borrowing.

- The average business can improve its odds of success greatly by getting paid in more than one way and at more than one time. You can do this with a variety of methods. (We'll cover this much more in Chapter 11.)

- Whether it's money, access to help, or anything else, you probably have more than you think. How can you get creative about finding what you need?

PART III

LEVERAGE AND NEXT STEPS

11 • Moving On Up

TWEAKING YOUR WAY TO THE BANK: HOW SMALL ACTIONS CREATE BIG INCREASES IN INCOME.

> **"Remind people that profit is the difference between revenue and expense. This makes you look smart."**
> **—SCOTT ADAMS**

Over and over, the subjects of our case studies discussed how growing the business wasn't nearly as hard as starting the business. "It took a while to find something that worked," a common statement began, "but once we were rolling, we gained traction and quickly took off."

As we saw with Nick's story in Chapter 6—the guy who was thrilled about selling his first $50 print—sometimes the first sale is the hardest but also the most rewarding. Several others said much the same thing: "The day I got my first sale was when I knew the business was going to work out. Everything that came afterward was reinforcement of the initial success."

I call it "the first $1.26 is the hardest" principle, because one day many years ago I made my first $1.26 with a new project while on a layover in Brussels. I couldn't afford a single Belgian waffle on the day's take, but I had a good feeling about the future. In this chapter, we'll look at ways to move on up by increasing income in an existing business.

How does this happen? No doubt there are a few different factors. Momentum is important, as is the ongoing attention of the business owner. The longer a microbusiness is around, with customers and onlookers saying good things about it, the more the word will spread. In addition to these natural factors, a series of small, regular actions is all it takes for many businesses to go from zero to hero in a short period of time. These actions are called tweaks.

• • •

Nev Lapwood was a classic ski bum. He lived in Whistler, British Columbia, and worked "off and on" in restaurants at night while snowboarding during the day. Life was basic but good . . . until the limited employment ended when Nev was laid off. Needing to make ends meet, he began offering snowboard lessons, a part-time gig that was highly valued by his students.

Teaching students in person on the Whistler slopes was fun and rewarding, but it also had a number of built-in unavoidable limitations: lots of competition, relatively few clients, and limited times of year when he could work. Nev knew that people all over the world wanted to learn about snowboarding—what if he could teach them all virtually, without needing to be in the same place? Getting his act together, Nev worked with a couple of close friends to create Snowboard Addiction, a worldwide series of snowboarding tutorials.

It was an instant hit, drawing customers from twenty countries and making $30,000 in year one—not bad for a ski bum. (Since Nev had never been that focused on making money, that was the highest annual income he had ever had at that point.) The next year, he put more thought into the business, scaling up with affiliates and a broader range of products. The result: just under $100,000 in net income. Nev was still on the slopes during the day but worked closely with his new partners during the downtimes to scale the business even further. The next plan was foreign language translation: Snowboard Addiction went out around the world in nine languages, with more versions scheduled to roll out based on customer demand.

Naturally, the growing business had its challenges. An untrained and accidental entrepreneur, Nev had to learn a lot about strategy, accounting, and marketing. Stickers that were ordered from China arrived months late and in an unusable condition. Just two years in, however, the business was on track to earn at least $300,000. As we've heard over and over in other stories, Nev speaks proudly of his new independence. "Frankly, starting this business after being laid off has been the best decision of my life," he says. "The greatest benefit has been the freedom and ability to do what I like. My plan is to travel for six months of every year and run the business for the other six months of each year." And of course, while he's running the business, he still finds plenty of time to hit the slopes.

Tweaking Your Way to the Bank: The Big Picture

The not-so-secret to improving income in an existing business is through *tweaks:* small changes that create a big impact. If a product typically has a 1.5 percent conversion rate and you increase the rate to 1.75 percent, the difference adds up to a lot of money as time goes on. If a business normally attracts four new customers a day and begins attracting five, the impact is tremendous. Not only is the business now earning 25 percent more income, it has diversified its customer base.*

If you grow your traffic *a little* and also increase your conversion

---

*I'm grateful to Sonia Simone and Brian Clark for a discussion and helpful tips on this topic.

rate *a little* while also increasing the average sales price *a little* . . . your business grows *a lot*. These are the most important areas on which to focus your tweak efforts, so let's look at them closely.

INCREASE TRAFFIC. Whether you have a website or a storefront, without people who regularly drop by to see your offer, you have no business. Traffic means *attention*. How much attention is your business getting? I heard from a new business owner who was disappointed in the results of her first product launch because only four people had purchased. "How many prospects were on your list?" I asked.

"I'm not entirely sure," she said. "Maybe one hundred?"

I said I was impressed, because 4 percent is a great conversion rate for many businesses. The problem wasn't getting more of her limited audience to purchase. It was getting more of an audience in the first place. The best thing to do in this situation is to focus on increasing traffic, thereby bringing in more potential customers.*

INCREASE CONVERSION. Once you have a stable base of attention (whether measured in site traffic or another way), you'll want to look closely at the conversion rate: the percentage of prospects who become customers. The classic way to increase the conversion rate is through testing by measuring one copywriting attempt (or offer, or headline, or something else) against another and going with the winner.

Traffic → A/B test → compare results

After you have a winner, you move on to another test, always challenging the "champion" against another idea. (Google Optimizer allows you to do this for free.)

---

*Corbett Barr maintains a helpful (and free) set of resources on building traffic at Think Traffic.net.

This can indeed be a good strategy. One tip, however: It may be more important to pay close attention to where customers come from than to what you can do to convert them once they arrive. "Testing is important, but it pales in comparison to the traffic source," author and entrepreneur Ramit Sethi told me. "People love to spend time split-testing headlines, copy, graphics, even tiny boxes. They can usually achieve greater returns by focusing on the source."

INCREASE AVERAGE SALES PRICE. If you can increase the average sales price per order, this will increase your bottom line, just as increasing traffic or conversion will. You can do this most easily through upsells, cross-sells, and sales after the sale. If you shop on Amazon.com, you've probably seen its "related items" and "customers who bought this item also bought these items" features. These features are highlighted (and widely replicated elsewhere) for a simple reason: They work extremely well.

The difference between upsells, cross-sells, and sales after the sale is illustrated below:

	How It Works	Message
Upsell	Offers a higher-level version or additional item upon purchase	"Would you like fries with that?"
Cross-sell	Offers "related items" to customers making a purchase	"Other people making this same purchase also bought these things."
Sale after the sale	Special offer made to customers immediately after a sale	"Thanks! This additional, one-time offer is *only* for customers."

(A good shopping cart and payment processor will allow you to add these items easily. If yours doesn't, it's time to change services.)

SELL MORE TO EXISTING CUSTOMERS. Your existing customers are likely to respond to sales, promotions, or additional offers of any kind. By reaching out to them more frequently, you'll almost certainly bring in additional income. You'll want to be careful about not pushing them too much, but the key is balance: Your customers *want* to hear from you. They have given you money in exchange for something they value. Make it easy for them to do so again and again.

Tweaking Your Way to the Bank: All the Details

When I talked with business owners about the kind of tweaks they worked on, many said things such as "The most important thing is to keep taking action." Others mentioned setting aside half an hour every morning to work strictly on business improvements before diving in to the actual running of the business. All of this sounds good, but it also begs the question: If you decide to take action, what does action look like? How do you spend your daily half hour on business improvements?

Here are some common examples of action-based tweaking.

CREATE A HALL OF FAME. Shine a spotlight on your best customers; let them tell their own stories about how they've been helped through your business. It helps to provide a variety of stories, as people will relate to different perspectives and backgrounds. This provides "social proof" that your product or service works for all kinds of people.

INSTITUTE A NEW UPSELL. Adding a good upsell offer—or several—is probably the easiest and most powerful strategy you can use to ramp up your average order size. Some business owners are initially apprehensive about upsells, not wanting to apply a high-pressure or "sleazy" technique. But a good upsell isn't sleazy at all; it's contextually appropriate and inspires appreciation from customers. "Wow, thanks for the offer!" is a common response. Think about going to a restaurant where you hadn't planned on eating dessert, but the waiter's recommendation of the chocolate bread pudding is so compelling that you have to try it . . . and it's delicious. You were successfully upsold, and you were happy about it.

The confirmation page that appears after an online purchase is one of the best and most underused places for an upsell offer. Right after a customer has purchased, they are highly inclined to purchase something else. Make a strong offer here, and your conversion rate can be 30 percent or higher.

ENCOURAGE REFERRALS. Most people know that word of mouth is the greatest source of new business, but instead of waiting for something to happen, you can encourage your customers to spread the word.* When asking for referrals, it helps to be specific: "Can you send our offer to three of your friends?" or "Can you 'like' our page on Facebook?" might be a good fit. Again, the confirmation page after a purchase is a good place to do this, in addition to a mailing sent a few days later.

HOLD A CONTEST. As mentioned in Chapter 9, some people become extremely motivated about contests and giveaways. Find a way to give away a prize and invite people to compete. The bigger the prize or the more unique the contest, the better. You may not make a ton of sales from a contest, but it will bring you more attention and a greater audience for future sales.

---

*John Jantsch wrote a great book called *The Referral Engine*, which is all about creating a systemized process for encouraging referrals. Highly recommended.

INTRODUCE THE MOST POWERFUL GUARANTEE YOU CAN THINK OF. Most businesses have boring guarantees: If you don't like this, you'll get your money back. But when we buy something, our money isn't all we're concerned with. We're also concerned about time and validation. If I have to return something, will it be a pain in the ass? Make it the opposite of a pain in the ass—some businesses provide a guarantee of 110 percent, ensuring that the burden is on the business to deliver. Zappos famously created free shipping *both* ways to take away the hesitation about buying shoes without trying them on. A host of competitors had to follow suit.*

ALTERNATIVELY, MAKE A BIG DEAL ABOUT OFFERING NO GUARANTEE. Instead of providing an incredible guarantee, provide *no* guarantee—and make a big deal about this fact. Note that this strategy usually works better for high-end products. It will likely decrease overall sales but increase the commitment level from those who do purchase.

Ironically, people who pay for high-end products tend to be better customers all around. "Low-paying buyers are the worst," one business owner who sold a broad range of products at different prices told me. "We have far more complaints from people who pay $10 and expect the world than from those who pay $1,000." I've noticed a similar effect in my own business, with people buying the lower-priced version of something generating a much higher rate of customer service issues than those who buy the higher-priced version.

---

*A little-known secret at Zappos is that they do cut people off who abuse the generous return policy. CEO Tony Hsieh explained to me that if a customer blatantly takes advantage of them—returning worn shoes on day 364 of the 365-day return period, for example—they'll honor the refund once, but they'll also gently advise that customer not to purchase from Zappos anymore. Fortunately, he also said, most people are honest.

The key lesson in all these ideas is to always be experimenting. Try new things and see what happens.

Product to Service, Service to Product

Another easy thing many existing businesses can do to add a new revenue source quickly is to create a service from a product-based business or create a product from a service-based business. Remember the story about the restaurant in Chapter 2? Most people go to a restaurant so they can relax and let the staff serve them. But others really are interested in how the cooking works, so restaurants sometimes offer cooking classes to show off their favorite recipes and create more loyalty among frequent diners. The key is that the lessons are held on Saturday or Sunday afternoons, times when the restaurant is closed or not very busy. Saturday night is reserved for the main event of regular dining.

If you have a product business, ask yourself this question: "My product is x . . . how can I teach customers about y?" Then create a new version of your offering that includes consulting, coaching, a "jump-start" session, premium technical support, or something else. Make it clear that customers don't *need* the service; they can get by on their own with just the product. But for those who are interested in some extra hand-holding, the service is available and waiting for them.

Perry Marshall, a Chicago-based business consultant, made the switch from product to service by offering an educational course based on knowledge he usually shared through a one-time product. Perry had written a popular report that sold multiple copies every day for $50 each. He was also busy offering one-on-one personal consulting, but one day someone gave him an idea: "Everyone who buys this report loves it, but they don't always know how to implement what you teach. They also don't need your high-end one-on-one consulting, so why not offer a series of jump-start workshops that people could take as a group?" Perry wasn't sure at first but decided to give it a try. When the idea generated more than a million dollars for his small firm, he was astounded.

Alternatively, if you operate a service-based business, consider how you can introduce a "productized" version of the service. My designer, Reese Spykerman, does work that is so great that when word got out, a lot of people began noticing and asking her for quotes. It didn't take long for Reese to have far more inquiries than she could handle. Reese's husband, Jason, manages the inquiries that come in every day, and he noticed that they fit into three categories.

Category 1: Prospects with significant money to spend who would likely be good clients. In these cases, Jason consulted with Reese, agreed to accept the clients if they still wished to proceed, and issued them a quote for the requested work.

Category 2: Prospects who didn't have any money to spend (designers receive a lot of these queries, unfortunately) or people who just weren't the right fit for Reese's work. In this case, Jason politely declined the request and encouraged them to look elsewhere.

These two categories were fairly straightforward, and as hundreds of inquires came in over the course of an average year, Jason became astute in telling right away which group someone was in. But there was another, third category that was more complicated.

Category 3: Prospects who had some money to spend, were nice people with interesting projects, and didn't need a completely custom solution.

The third category was complicated because Reese and Jason didn't want to send them away, but they also didn't want to take on an excessive number of projects, thus limiting Reese's design time for key clients. They did some careful subcontracting, but they didn't want to become a low-end provider or farm out much of the work to others.

After considering different options, Reese and Jason decided to create a series of "themes" and website headers that customers could purchase for a flat rate. These options weren't the same as a genuinely custom-crafted site design, but they were a lot better than everything else on the market.

Providing both a product and a service helps with your marketing as well. You can say to prospects, "Hey, my service costs a lot of money because everything is customized. But if you just need a general solution, you can get this version for much less." Some customers will still want the customized solution, but this way you don't shut the door on others who like the idea but can't afford the high-end work.

What Sets Happy Knits Apart:
AN EXAMINATION OF A THRIVING RETAIL PRACTICE

How does a retail establishment thrive when those around it struggle? Welcome to Happy Knits, a yarn store and Internet retailer based in the trendy Southeast area of Portland, Oregon. Here are five ways Happy Knits stands out.

A welcoming space. Knitters are welcome to stay for hours, whether shopping or knitting. Guests who happen to be accompanying knitters—usually husbands or children—are also welcome to hang out, sit in comfy chairs, and use the free WiFi while the knitter of the family looks around. (Most, though not all, knitters are women.)

A clear online strategy. Most retail stores have a website, but few combine a physical location with an online shopping experience as well as Happy Knits does. "Online is limitless," says store owner Sarah Young. Even with a large retail space, online sales from around the world constitute more than half the sales. She works the system by maintaining close ties with Ravelry, a social network specifically for knitters, and providing frequent email updates and offers to previous customers.

Great displays (in store) and great photos (online). Display, color, and placement are important, so Happy Knits includes a staging area for professional photos in a back room of the store. I asked Sarah why she doesn't just use the photos provided by the manufacturer the way other stores do. "Because they're not good enough," she told me. "We try to do everything here with a focus on quality."

Exclusive deals. By working with yarn companies as partners, Happy Knits creates exclusivity that is hard to emulate. You might think this is an unfair advantage, but the companies offered these deals to Sarah because her customers said such good things about the store and because she is careful to pay vendors on time. (Lesson: To get an unfair advantage, provide remarkable service.)

Love for customers. Every order sent by mail includes a personalized thank-you note from an employee, encouraging customers to call if they need help with a pattern, plus free samples of other products. If an item is back ordered because of a computer glitch, an employee will call the customer proactively to apologize and ask if she would like a substitution.

"Be nice to people and provide a great service" may not sound like much of a differentiation, but all these things add up. Whether you have a retail store or not, you could learn something from Happy Knits.

Note to Service Providers: Raise Prices Regularly

You might expect that a price increase has a tendency to filter some customers away from the business while making up for the loss with higher overall income. Sometimes this is indeed the case, but many of the service providers I talked with were surprised that almost no one left after an increase. Several said that when they told their customers or clients about the increase, the response was, "It's about time! You're worth more than you've been charging." (When your clients complain about the price being too low, you should listen.)

Andy Dunn is a developer in Belfast, Northern Ireland. He left his day job after pitching a Web application to a CEO. Crucially, Andy didn't just pitch an idea—he had the idea and then acted on it by creating the entire app and sending it over to the CEO, requesting approval. Impressed, the CEO called him up to say thanks, and even agreed to underwrite the expenses for some additional features.

Out on his own, Andy had no problem attracting new business, but he did have a big problem with pricing. Wanting to appear attractive to prospective clients, he priced his services so low that they were unprofitable. In one case he ended up several thousand euros in debt by bidding too low and then outsourcing part of the work. After that experience, he knew he'd have to make a change. The change came in the form of a 25 percent raise, something he was initially afraid to do, but he was greatly relieved after it was done.

"The simple act of raising my rates by 25 percent allowed me to either work seven hours less a week or make a significant increase in my monthly income," he told me on a Skype call from Belfast. "The other, unexpected benefit was that it gave me much more confidence. Until I upped the rates, I didn't make the connection that I was worth more than I had been charging."

Andy's story was repeated in various forms by other service providers and a few product-based businesses too. In 2010 I conducted a separate study of fourteen freelancers who had raised their rates successfully. I asked them how they did it, what they expected to happen, and what actually happened. These freelancers were working in completely different fields, including a veterinarian, a voice coach, a sign language interpreter, and the more typical crowd of consultants, writers, and designers. They were also located throughout the English-speaking world, including Canada, Australia, New Zealand, South Africa, the United Kingdom, and the United States.

Despite the diverse backgrounds and regions, I heard the same story over and over: "Before my price increase, I was worried that no one would hire me again. After the price increase, I realized how easy it was, and I wish I had done it sooner." In most cases, the change was anticlimactic. Clients said, "OK, sure," and moved on.

I also asked about suggestions for other service providers who are thinking about raising their rates. The most common advice was to maintain a practice of regular rate increases so that it becomes normal and expected. One freelancer likened it to going to the grocery store: No one expects the price of milk to be the same from year to year. We all know that over time it's going to go up, and the same should be true for the prices we charge clients. Another suggested an annual date for changing prices, either January 1 or the beginning of your calendar year if it's different. Others said that they offered an ongoing discount for current clients, among whom the work is more familiar and a strong relationship already exists.

Lastly, remember to price on the basis of value, not time. One

designer sent us a good example of what *not* to do: "I have a col-
league who moderates her rate according to how busy the day was
and how long her lunch break was. Crazy!" Our correspondent is
right: Customers pay for what you deliver, not how long you spend
at lunch.

The Best Social Media Strategy: Talk About Yourself

You may have heard that the way to build a following on Twitter or other
social networks is to promote other people's work. People don't want to
hear you talk about yourself all the time, right?

This advice is well-meaning and sounds good on the surface. Unfortunately, it's also wrong. Promoting other people's work and sharing
links to interesting articles is fine, but don't expect that merely doing
that will help you gain followers or attention. People follow you (or your
business) because that's what they're interested in—*you*. I follow Sha-
quille O'Neal's tweets and posts because I'm interested in what he has
to say. If he spent all his time talking about other people and mentioning his other fans, I wouldn't be as interested.

What should you talk about online? It's simple: Talk about yourself
and your business. Really. If people don't like what you do or say, they
can unfollow you, but chances are that you'll gain far more followers
than you lose. Finally, remember that online social networks are merely
reflections of what's happening elsewhere. Want more Twitter followers?
Then do something interesting . . . away from Twitter.

A Cautionary Note

There's no point pursuing growth for growth's sake; you should
scale a business only if you really want to. Many of the subjects of
our case studies said they had turned down growth opportunities in

a deliberate plan to remain small: "I just didn't want the hassle of managing people."

The decision on going big versus staying small is unique to each person (we'll look at it much more in the next two chapters), but in this section we want to focus on things you can do to increase income *without* hiring additional employees or bringing in outside investors. All the tweaks mentioned above can be done by a solopreneur. Some might be easier with assistants, contractors, or employees, but none require a team. Before we close it out, let's look at a key distinction between two different kinds of growth.

You can grow a business one of two ways: horizontally, by going wide and creating different products to apply to different people, or vertically, by going deep and creating more levels of engagement with customers. The flowchart on page 201 shows how this works.

Different businesses will find that one solution suits them better than the other, and it's also possible to pursue limited growth in both areas. Mostly, though, you can keep moving on up, tweaking your way to the bank and growing your business. The first $1.26—or the first sale—may be the hardest, but after that, your most difficult choice may be deciding between many good options for growth.

KEY POINTS

- "Moving on up" by increasing income in an existing business is usually easier than initially starting the business.
- By making careful choices, you can often grow the business without dramatically increasing the workload, allowing you to scale without hiring more people.

- Easy growth options include adding a service to a product-based business (or vice versa), deploying a creative series of upsells and cross-sells, and making a few key tweaks.

- Horizontal expansion involves going *broader* by serving more customers with different (usually related) interests; vertical expansion involves going *deeper* by serving the same customers with different levels of need.

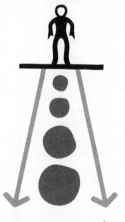

INSTRUCTIONS ON CLONING YOURSELF
FOR FUN AND PROFIT.

> "I'm not a businessman;
> I'm a business, man."
>
> —JAY-Z

As business models go, buying a franchise that is based on someone else's company is usually a bad idea. The basic buy-our-franchise pitch runs like this: Raise a quarter of a million dollars by withdrawing your life savings, borrowing from family members, and maxing out your credit cards. Pay most of that money up front to a company that will generously allow you to work for it. Operate the business precisely the way they tell you, with no exceptions allowed. Every decision, from whom you hire to what services you offer to where you locate your store, is made by the company. They'll even tell you what color shirt you are required to wear in "your own business."

If the business succeeds, you'll make an average of $47,000 a year after scraping by for three years on the same fifty-hour workweeks you could spend at someone else's company with a lot less stress. In this winning scenario, your ultimate success won't be that you started a business: You'll have bought yourself a job.

If the business fails, which happens more often than mo~ chise companies want to admit, the company will tak~

store from you and resell it to someone else. When they do this, they won't count your failure as a store closure in their statistics. Thus, when you hear statistics that suggest a high percentage of franchise locations remain open, you have no idea who is operating them and who owes $250,000 that they have no way to repay.

How does that proposal sound to you? Probably not so great— which is why buying into someone else's operation isn't usually the opportunity it may seem from the outside. Thankfully, there's an alternative: building a real business of your own, something that you have ownership of and control over. Buying into someone else's franchise isn't usually a good idea, but figuring out how to leverage your own efforts is almost always worth careful consideration.

You're Only One Person ... or Maybe Two

Who says you can't be in more than one place at one time? In fact, there are several ways to grow a business through the use of *leverage*. Franchising yourself isn't just doing more; it's about taking your skills, activities, and passions to a higher level to create better returns. The difference between franchising yourself and just doing more is that you take the time to be strategic. Let's look at a couple of examples.

Nathalie Lussier was an up-and-coming software engineer. Originally from Quebec, she had interned in Silicon Valley and now had the chance to take a big job on Wall Street. Her family said it was the job of her dreams . . . but as Nathalie thought more about it, she realized it was the job of someone else's dreams. Turning down the offer, she returned to Canada and decided to pursue a different idea.

Nathalie had a personal success story of dramatically improving her health after switching to a raw foods diet. Eating only fruits, vegetables, and nuts sounded crazy at first, but the results spoke for themselves: In the first month, she lost more than ten pounds and suddenly had energy throughout the day. As she talked with her friends, Nathalie was a natural evangelist—not pushy or judgmental, but offering tips and strategies that people could use to make real improvements even if they weren't ready to jump into a completely raw diet as Nathalie had done.

After relocating to Toronto, the idea was to build a small business helping other people make the adjustment to raw foods. Being a software engineer (and a self-described geek like Brett Kelly in Chapter 4), Nathalie programmed a database, set up an app, and built her own website. The first incarnation was Raw Food Switch, which correctly represented the concept but seemed a bit boring. One day Nathalie noticed that the same letters—and therefore the same website—could be rendered as Raw Foods Witch, leading to a new theme. Dressing in character with a pointed black hat for photo shoots, she rebranded the whole business around herself. Nathalie created programs, one-time products, and individual consultation sessions in the same way we've seen others do throughout the book. Raw Foods Witch grew into a $60,000 business after the first year.

What's not to love? Just one thing: "From the outside," she told me at a vegetarian restaurant in Toronto, "it looked like all I talked about was raw foods. No one realized I had done all the programming and really enjoyed the intersection of business and technology."

The second business came about unexpectedly after Nathalie began getting tech inquiries from her raw foods clients who were also creating businesses. She decided to create a separate brand for tech consulting, operating under her own name instead of the moniker she used in the other business. Raw Foods Witch is still a powerful brand—friends and clients report that other shoppers have mentioned her in the grocery store when they see a cart full of avocados—but she restructured the business to run on 80 percent autopilot. It still brings in a good income, but now Nathalie spends her time building the second business. Instead of doing one or the other, Nathalie effectively franchised herself.

After Nathalie set up the tech consultancy, she had to go back to the raw foods business and make some changes. The business had always been dependent on new products and launches, and since her focus was now elsewhere, she had to reduce that dependency while ensuring that it would produce income on a more regular basis.

Across the border and a few states away, Brooke Thomas founded New Haven Rolfing, a holistic health practice. The clinic attracts a clearly defined group of clients: people who want to address chronic pain and mobility problems. (No one comes to see Brooke when they're feeling great.) By the time they arrive at New Haven Rolfing, many have gone through a long list of other treatments that haven't helped. Brooke is a testimony to the treatment she provides—she became pain-free through Rolfing after twenty-three years, having lived her whole life to that point with problems related to a birth injury.

Before she moved to Connecticut, Brooke operated similar businesses in California and New York. With each move she learned a little more about what to do and what to avoid. Opening the same kind of business in different cities was insightful. After moving to New Haven, she had filled her client list within four weeks, and then she took on a partner to manage additional appointments. A single mother with a young child, Brooke works part-time but still earns more than $70,000 a year from the practice.

Repeated success in different cities involved getting to know other care providers, and Brooke noticed that some were more business-savvy than others. By using her real-world experience, Brooke created Practice Abundance, a training program for other wellness providers. Offering a series of support modules and a community forum, Practice Abundance was a business course that focused strictly on ways to improve a practice. Other resources took a very traditional approach. In Brooke's words, "they assume that everyone wants to get an MBA, when the reality is that most of them just want to run their practice better." Brooke had diversified to two groups of people: those she served through individual care, and her fellow caregivers who could benefit from non–MBA business advice.

• • •

Both Nathalie and Brooke found a way to reach two different audiences: a core group and a related group. As a business grows and the business owner begins itching for new projects, he or she essentially has two options for self-made franchising:

Option 1: Reach more people with the same message.
Option 2: Reach different people with a new message.

Either option is valid, and both can be rewarding. For the first option, it may be helpful to think of the "hub-and-spoke" model when building a brand, especially online. In this model, the hub is your main website: often an e-commerce site where something is sold, but it could also be a blog, a community forum, or something else. The hub is a home base with all the content curated by you or your team and ultimately where you hope to drive new visitors, prospects, and customers.

The spokes, also known as *outposts*, are all the other places where you spend your time.* These places could include social networking sites, the comments section of your blog or other blogs, actual meetings or networking events, or something else. You can see how this works in the image below:

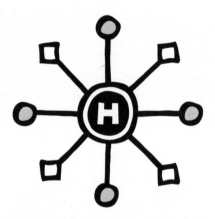

Hub and Spoke Model

The goal for each of the outposts is to support the work of the home base, not usually the outpost itself. It can be a trap to spend too much time with any of the outposts, because things change, some outposts become less popular over time. You also own the content and work you create in the home base, whereas most of what happens in an outpost is "owned" by another company.

---

*I'm grateful to Chris Brogan for the term *outposts* as well as the general concept of the hub and spoke applied to building a brand. Darren Rowse and Chris Garrett also contributed to this conversation.

Disaster and Recovery:
"STUCK IN MALI AGAIN" EDITION

As a full-time freelance photographer based in Accra, Ghana, Nyani Quarmyne is no stranger to adventure. In West Africa, there are few laws that are widely followed, especially when it comes to copyright and intellectual property. Most of the time, everything works out—but not always. Here's how Nyani tells the story:

When I was just starting out, I shot a couple of small jobs for a Ghanaian creative agency. Shortly thereafter I got a call from them asking if I could do an urgent shoot for a new client, necessitating travel to a couple of countries in the region. The deadline was really tight; it was a get-the-call-today-and-leave-in-the-morning kind of thing, and even the details of exactly where we would be going remained in flux until the last minute. Having shot for the agency before, they had seen and signed my contracts previously, and I made the mistake of thinking they understood how I work and the basis on which I was undertaking this job. So in the rush I omitted to get the paperwork squared away, and off we went.

The shoot went really well, and I produced what I consider to be some very strong work. All was well until we were on a rural road far from any city or airport. While we were driving along, the client demanded copyright of the images—not part of the deal as far as I was concerned—and threatened to have me detained at a remote border in a politically unstable nation unless I handed them over. Not wanting to sample the hospitality of the local gendarmes, I conceded and lost some of the strongest images I had shot to date. I learned my lesson, though: Next time, be sure to get the paperwork done first.

Partnership: How 1 + 1 = 3

One path to franchising yourself is to team up with a trusted partner. This doesn't mean you completely merge your business with that person; in fact, the easiest and most common way to partner with someone is to create a *joint venture*. In this arrangement, two or more people join forces to collaborate on a single new project. (Karol and Adam's "fire sale" project, described in Chapter 8, is a joint venture.)

In other arrangements, an all-new business is created that is jointly owned by the partners. That's what Patrick McCrann and Rich Strauss did. They were both high-end performance coaches for athletes and decided to team up to create Endurance Nation, a training program and community for triathletes. They divide responsibilities on the basis of what they're each good at. Patrick calls all the new members on the phone to welcome them, and Rich crafts an online training plan for them.*

However it's structured, the goal of a partnership is to grow beyond what each person can create on his or her own. Ralf Hildebrandt operates an international professional services firm based in Stuttgart, Germany. Here's how he explains why 1 + 1 can equal 3: "My rule of thumb is that a successful partnership (or any type of collaboration) should create a combined business which is at least 33 percent larger than the sum of what the two individuals could achieve on their own.

"People are often inclined to think that distributing work to a few others is what partnership is about," Ralf continued. "But that is just subcontracting. True partnership must create more than just a divided list of tasks."

---

*Patrick and Rich use a good cop-bad cop routine in handling their business, which relates well to their differences: Patrick was in the Peace Corps and Rich was in the Marine Corps. Patrick has kids and lives on the East Coast; Rich is childless and lives on the West Coast.

Courtesy of Pamela Slim, a coach, author, and expert on partnerships, here's an abbreviated list of decisions you should make at the beginning of any joint venture:

- How will the money be divided? (Common splits include an even 50-50, 60-40 with the higher share going to the partner who does more work, and 45-45 with 10 percent reserved for administrative costs.)
- What are the responsibilities of each partner?
- What kind of information is shared between partners?
- How will the project be jointly marketed?
- How long will our agreement be in place?
- How often will we touch base to discuss the partnership?

Check out the One-Page Partnership Agreement for a simple way to spell out basic agreements between two parties.

One-Page Partnership Agreement

Keep it simple. Remember that the relationship is the most important part; choosing to keep it strong and trusting is more important than having the right clauses and legal language. Many of our subjects report doing business for large amounts of money on a long-term basis without any contracts at all. Here's a starting point. You should consult a qualified third party if you'd like to define your obligations more clearly or if you're concerned about something.

Partners: [Partner 1] and [Partner 2]. These partners agree to collaborate in good faith on a mutually beneficial project known as [project name].

Overview: [summary of project, including outcomes and expected results]

Revenue Sharing: Net income for the project will be split on the basis of [percentage] percent to [Partner 1] and [percentage] percent to [Partner 2]. All minor costs associated with the project will be deducted prior to calculating net income. If any particular cost exceeds [amount], both partners must approve the decision.

Life of Revenue-Sharing Agreement: The revenue-sharing agreement will last for [period of time], at the end of which the partners will decide if it should be continued, discontinued, or revised.

Publication and Sale: The project will be offered for sale on [websites and any other sources].

Customer Support: [Partner 1] will be responsible for [duties]. [Partner 2] will be responsible for [duties]. Project feedback from customers will be shared between both parties.

Marketing: Both parties will actively market the project to ensure its success. This will include promotion on [websites], through each partner's online community and offline networks, and each party requesting coverage of the project from other influential websites.

Time Line: The partners agree to complete all aspects of the project to prepare for launch on [date].

The Battle of Outsourcing

Jamila Tazewell followed a common path after graduating from art school: She waited tables in New York City while dreaming of something else. Fortunately, waiting on tables was the only waiting she did—she also took action to start a business. She started by making "outlandish handbags" and unique wallets. "I was convinced I would magically become an accessories star overnight," she says, initially assuming that a fashion house would see her products and offer to distribute them. "Then I saw I could actually sell my handbags and wallets myself. That's when I decided to pursue the opportunity further."

Jamila headed west to Los Angeles to sell her accessories full-time without relying on a waitress job to pay the bills this time. It worked, but only just barely: She did everything herself, and the business struggled to find its feet. She was glad she no longer waited tables, but as with buying someone else's franchise, Jamila felt like she bought herself a job.

Three years in, Jamila was ready to make a change. She hired a local seamstress to make the product under her supervision, a move she describes as "challenging but necessary." After that, she brought in someone to do the printing and shipping as well. This was a big step that required "a brutal process of trial and error, but getting the product out of my home office was incredibly liberating. It felt like my child was finally old enough to go off to boarding school or something."

Interestingly, this perspective is not universally accepted. Several other topics covered in the study resulted in a wave of similar responses. Many members of our group spoke of bootstrapping and limited business plans in the same way, and the connection between freedom and value was a key theme for almost everyone. But there was one topic that resulted in a wave of divergent opinions. That topic was employing contractors or "virtual assistants," also known as *outsourcing*. On this topic, input ranged from "love it" to "hate it" to "it's complicated."

For every story like Jamila's that told of partnership leading to freedom, I heard a contrasting story from someone who was much happier deliberately keeping the business to themselves, without outsourcing or hiring. Let's look at a few examples of the different camps.

CASE 1: PRO-OUTSOURCING

The camp in favor of outsourcing can be represented with the following statements from business owners who came to view their release from tasks and responsibility as a freeing decision:

> Hiring employees was my biggest challenge as a business owner. I put it off for years and turned away tens of thousands of dollars each year because I was afraid to grow. Finally, I realized that I had hit a ceiling. I couldn't make any more money without bringing some members to my team. Since changing the structure, I'm able to accept all of the orders I had had to turn away. I'm no longer overbooked, and I can invest extra time in moving the business forward in other aspects. Do I wish I could do it all myself? I used to, because I don't like to lead or be led. I don't like to feel like the boss. But I am so much happier now as part of a team. I'm the pilot of my business, and my crew is there to make my work easier while fulfilling their own goals as well. —Megan Hunt (*read more about Megan in Chapter 3*)

> Our aim has always been to have zero employees in order to avoid the expense, complex legal issues, and inflexibility. However, our warehousing operation is completely contracted out—all stock receipts, storage, processing, pick, pack, and dispatch is taken care of by our logistics partners; we just send the orders. We use freelance sales agents, who are paid on commission only. We use virtual assistants for telephone answering when we are unavailable. —Jonathan Pincas (*read more about Jonathan in Chapter 14*)

> We contracted with an outside printer to make our first run of maps, and it was the best decision we have ever made. Our business would literally not exist if we had tried to print the

maps on our own. As demand has increased, our printers have been able to provide us with additional inventory. We never would have been able to print large quantities of posters while maintaining our full-time jobs and tending to a growing business. We are also happy that our business can support the work of other artisans. —Jen Adrion and Omar Noory (*read more about Jen and Omar in Chapter 6*)

These quotes are representative of others who have all said similar things: Outsourcing increases freedom and allows a business to scale without the owners doing everything themselves.

CASE 2: ANTI-OUTSOURCING

The camp opposed to outsourcing can be represented with the following statements from business owners who believed that expansion would be difficult, undesirable, or otherwise limiting of the freedom they had achieved through the business:

I'm at the point where I need to find a way to grow my ability to respond to customer demand, but I struggle with concerns over reputation to the extent that I turn over bookings to employees or contractors. I've been offered partnerships, but I turn them down because either I have concerns over the quality of the partner or because the partner wants a referral commission. I could easily raise my price and provide the commission, but I know I wouldn't be happy working for less. And thus I haven't grown further, though I'm comfortable with that for now. —Gary Leff (*read more about Gary in Chapter 3*)

I actually prefer not to work with contractors, employees, or assistants. My business succeeds on the fact that it is intentionally small. I can fit my whole business into a backpack and take it wherever I go—no office, no stationery, no administrative staff. Keeping my overhead to zero has lowered the risks and kept profits high. —Adam Westbrook (*Adam operates a design services business from the United Kingdom*)

I'm big on keeping the company lean and mean. I'm the only employee, and I work out of my home. We used to own a retail business where paying rent, insurance, and twelve employees came ahead of our own paychecks. Those days are over. Simply put, I don't like getting paid last. —Jaden Hair (*read more about Jaden in Chapter 2*)

My experiences with outsourcing work to remote contractors left me spending nearly as much time managing the work as it would to actually do it myself. I've yet to find a nice balance of being able to hire someone to work on a project and making a reasonable profit without spending too much time on it myself. —Andy Dunn (*read more about Andy in Chapter 11*)

My motto: Never have a boss and never be a boss. Since age twenty-two, this has been my situation. I have an accountant, because number crunching is my biggest weakness. Otherwise, I am a company of one. I can always vouch for my own work, and my integrity means the world to me. —Brandy Agerbeck (*read more about Brandy in Chapter 7*)

As with the pro-outsourcing camp, these quotes are representative of many others. Lee Williams-Demming mentioned that her importing business formerly had five employees and hundreds of overseas suppliers. It now has only one employee and a smaller supplier network. "Trust me," she wrote in an email, "we're better off in every way with a much smaller team."

• • •

Although I know it's not the best fit for everyone, I tend to fall into the anti-outsourcing camp in my own business. Instead of sending out projects to everywhere, I've chosen to keep a very small team and do only limited contracting with outsiders. The first argument for outsourcing is that it allows you as a business owner to "do more of what you love" while assigning unwanted tasks to someone else. But outsourcing can create greater problems, and you can construct your business in a way in which few of these tasks are actually needed in the first place.

More than once, I've heard from colleagues who say they have a fantastic virtual assistant they'd be happy to recommend to me. Then, weeks or months later, I hear they're looking for a new one. "What happened to so-and-so?" I ask. "Well, they were great . . . at first. But then the process broke down, balls were dropped, and we had to part ways."

This is a recurring story, told many ways but with the same end result. There are certainly exceptions, but many capable people who work as virtual assistants often end up deciding they'd rather be running their own show. If you have to spend your time correcting problems caused by the team created to support you, the team hasn't really improved your life. Meanwhile, it's clear that others have definitely benefited from harnessing the "get other people to do your stuff" wave.

With such divergent opinions, how do you know which path to follow? Thankfully, it's not that complicated. The answer to the question of whether outsourcing is a good fit depends on two things: (1) the specific business and (2) the personality of the business owner.

Many of the problems people experience with outsourcing (on

both sides) can be avoided by having a clear understanding of the responsibilities that a contractor or assistant will have. In a business that relies on a series of relatively mindless, repetitive tasks, for example, outsourcing may be a good option. A business that relies on customer relationships, however, may not be a good fit.

Your own personality also matters, because if you're building a freedom business, you want to find the best possible solution to match your vision of freedom. For some people, that involves traveling the world on a low-overhead operation, with the money from the business primarily going to support the owner. Other people want to stay in one place and build a team, creating a business that will outlast themselves. In the end, the best answer to the outsourcing question is the same as many others: Do what makes sense for you, not for someone else.

Barter, Family Help, and Housecleaning

Before we move on, let's look at a couple of other forms of getting help. "My entire business is a product of extremely beneficial trades," says Brooke Snow, who traded music lessons for photography lessons before going on to teach photography herself. She also traded for website design, video footage, and tech support. "These trades have saved me tens of thousands of dollars and have not only transformed my business but are in many ways some of the very reasons I have a business. It has allowed me to operate completely debt free with low financial investment, low overhead, and a high rate of return."

Several respondents mentioned that other tasks were "outsourced" to family members. After every $1,000 milestone in Eleanor Mayrhofer's stationery business, she makes a special dinner for her husband, who helps out with bookkeeping and programming. Nathalie Lussier mentioned that hiring a housecleaner made a big difference in her productivity. "Although that might seem trivial," she wrote, "it was actually key to realizing how important it is not to try to do it all myself all the time." Jonathan Pincas wrote in with a last-minute correction to his earlier comments on outsourcing: He wanted to note that his mother gets the mail twice a week in England and then scans it to forward it electronically.

The Business Audit

However it is structured, a good business needs nurturing and con-tinuous improvement. As your project grows, take some time to look at each aspect of it, especially any public communication that customers review while making a purchasing decision. Answer these questions and think about how you can improve. The goal is to (1) fix little problems and (2) identify small actions you can take that will create significant results over time.

"WHERE DO YOU MAKE MONEY?"

Once a business gets up and running, it's very easy to get trapped in all kinds of things that have nothing to do with making money. The solution is simple: Focus on the money. In the audit, you'll want to look at where the money comes from and determine what you can do to keep it coming. Sometimes new opportunities present themselves; sometimes there's an easy fix you can make to turn on another tap. If you have a range of projects, products, or activities, it's almost always better to devote your efforts to the strong performers than to try and pull up the weak ones. Most people do the opposite, but if your goal is for everything to be average, that's the best you'll ever get.

"HOW GOOD IS YOUR MESSAGING?"

The marketing materials you use, whether online or offline, probably involve some use of words, known as *copy*. Go back to the beginning and read the copy carefully. Review each page of the sales material slowly and then read it out loud. Does it still present the message that you want? What information should be culled or revised?

"ARE YOUR PRICES WHAT THEY SHOULD BE?"

When was the last time you raised your prices? You can have a sale or give out discount codes from time to time, but like all businesses, you should also plan on raising your prices on a regular basis as well. Always remember that trying to price for "everyone" is a business death trap. Since business owners live or die by the free market system, the way you decide whether your pricing is fair is by asking another question: Are people buying what you sell? If the answer is yes, you're on the right track. If it is no, you have a problem.

"HOW ARE YOU MARKETING TO EXISTING CUSTOMERS?"

One of the best things you can do is reach out to existing customers and find a way to meet more of their needs. As part of this examination, you should check your postpurchase process carefully. What happens after someone buys? Do things get sent to the right place? Does everything arrive in the buyer's in-box or physical mailbox as it should? If you sell consulting, do clients know exactly how to set up a time in your schedule after making a payment? The easier you can make all of these things, the better.

"ARE YOU TRACKING, MONITORING, OR TESTING ENOUGH?"

The thing about testing is that you just don't know what's going to happen until you do it. That's why you test! Once I installed an upsell offer in which customers could get a $50 gift certificate for only $25 after making a purchase. I thought it was a killer offer, but my customers didn't think so; it was accepted only one out of twenty times (5 percent). A good upsell can convert much better than that, so out went the gift certificate offer.

> **"WHERE ARE THE BIG MISSING OPPORTUNITIES?"**
>
> Having a big opportunity doesn't mean you should pursue it. I pass up a lot of things because they aren't a good fit for my overall strategy. However, it's good to know what you're missing even if you're missing it deliberately. Keep your "possibilities list" updated so you can follow up when you have more time or if you need more money.

In Murfreesboro, Tennessee, Erica Cosminsky was a human resources professional for a pharmacy chain and a parent to two-year-old Riley. Working long hours during the day, she traded off child care with Riley's father, with Erica taking the weekend shift while he took the weekdays. When she was unexpectedly laid off, the shock gradually turned to relief—Erica had been thinking about starting a service company but never had the time.

The goal was to operate a small transcription service, typing up the contents of conference calls, interviews, and meetings for other businesses. Erica first had the idea to provide her service in real time, attending live conferences, typing on the fly, and delivering the contents before the end of the day. She was good at the jobs she took under this arrangement, but there were two problems: Live conference work was scarce, and it interfered with her child care needs.

Erica was worried about competing as a basic transcription service, since many other companies already performed that role. Live transcription wasn't the best differentiator, but Erica found another: adding basic formatting and a nice-looking layout to the transcriptions she delivered. Most competitors refused to do any design whatsoever, making clear that their job was just to transcribe. Many of Erica's clients were solopreneurs or other very small businesses, and not everyone had access to a graphic designer or layout person who could take over after receiving a transcription. The differentiation worked; within three months of reversing course and putting out the word that she was available, Erica could no longer keep up and was ready to expand the team.

Then she made another key decision: not to hire employees but only hire contractors. By building the team on a contract-only basis, she had more flexibility to increase or downsize the numbers, depending on market needs. This was important because of the way the industry works: From November to May in a recent cycle, she was completely booked up and had to recruit seventeen transcriptionists serving 180 clients, plus a virtual assistant to keep everyone on track. But in the summertime, very few businesses need transcription work, so the team shrinks to four people. (The contractors all understand that the work is cyclical and future projects aren't guaranteed.)

These days Erica manages the business without doing any actual transcription herself. She has created a flexible structure that allows her to respond to the market without feeling locked in or overloaded by doing it all herself. The business experienced a testing point in the fall of 2009, when Erica's daughter contracted a bad case of the flu, requiring Erica to spend almost her whole time as a caregiver for three weeks. It was hard to deal with on a personal level, she says, but fortunately, the team was there to back her up and most of the business clients didn't even realize she was gone. Riley recovered, and Erica went back to work, leaving her delayed on invoices but thankfully not delayed on actual income. The model of team building through contractors worked.

Affiliate Programs: The Good, the Bad, and the Lifeless

You may be familiar with affiliate programs, in which merchants cooperate with partners to bring in more traffic and sales, rewarding affiliates with a cut of the earnings. Although a few other businesses had experimented with this model earlier, Amazon.com started the first mainstream "associates" partnership back in 1996, inviting its customers to join as revenue-sharing partners.

Since then, almost every major retailer has come up with some kind of affiliate program, as have many small businesses of all kinds. You can start your own affiliate program very easily (a four-step startup guide is available for free at 100startup.com), and this can be an easy way to franchise yourself. Do it right, and hundreds of eager affiliates will line up to promote your work. Do it better, though, and you'll create a true partnership that will bring you steady income over time no matter what else is happening in your business or the general economy.

It works like this:

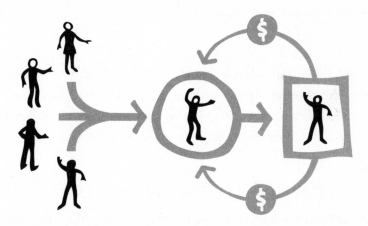

Visitors ➝ **Affiliate** ➝ **Merchant**

There are two big problems with most affiliate programs. First, the merchants tend to pay very small commissions, leaving little for the affiliate who sent them the referral in the first place, and second, the affiliates tend to do no more than blindly pass over referrals. Big problems create big opportunities, so a good merchant can offer a better program by paying much higher commissions to start with but also expecting more from the affiliate.

For years I've paid a 51 percent commission to affiliates in my business under the principle that they should earn more than I do for promoting my work. At the same time, I make it clear that they'll need to do more than just slap up a link somewhere. If they want to be successful, they'll need to create a closer connection between their readers and my business. They can do that by using the products themselves, writing reviews, and offering some kind of bonus to the referrals they make. If you structure your affiliate program in a similar manner, you'll attract higher-quality partners.

• • •

Partnerships and outsourcing can be a good way to build some businesses, but relying on someone else doesn't always work out as planned. Let's look at a (very) small business that did not benefit from a contract arrangement.

The Rise and Fall of Copley Trash Services

Spencer and Hannah Copley, ages twelve and ten, lived with their parents on board a hospital ship deployed to West Africa. Four hundred other adults (some with children) also lived on the ship, which spent six months at a time bringing surgeons and medical teams to countries such as Sierra Leone and Liberia.

Living on a ship in West Africa presented a number of challenges.

What might be small concerns at home quickly became real issues on an old ship deployed to a poor country. Particular to our story, everyone was responsible for taking out their own garbage, but it wasn't always an easy task. A large dumpster was located at the edge of the dock, requiring a long walk under the hot sun. Often the dumpster was full, and everyone had to keep their garbage in their small cabins until dumpster use became available again, sometimes several days later.

An entrepreneur in the making, twelve-year-old Spencer hit on an idea: What if he started a garbage collection service? The price was a steal. For just $1 a week, you could leave your garbage in the hall on Tuesdays and Fridays, and the tag team duo of Spencer and Hannah would be responsible for hauling it out to the dumpster. Spencer made a poster advertising the offer and tacked it to the bulletin board by the snack bar. The offer was an immediate hit: Ten customers signed up right away, and another fifteen in the next few weeks.

Having acquired a strong customer base, Spencer and Hannah made sure to keep their clients regularly informed with important updates. One day the dumpster was completely out of commission, and customers received a notice: "We regret to inform you that Copley Trash Services will not be open this Friday. We will perform an extra pickup on Sunday instead. Have a great day!" Another time, a leaky garbage bag created difficulties for ten-year-old Hannah, so a customer notice went out titled "Important Things to Know about Your Trash."*

Spencer and Hannah had created recurring income of $25 a week, a substantial preteen wage that was spent in three ways: Ten

---

*I was a customer of Copley Trash Services, and one week I neglected to pay my dues. A polite note was placed on my door: "Did you forget something?" I shamefully paid up and included an extra 50 cents in late fees.

percent went out as a tithe to an orphanage they had been visiting on the weekends, and 40 percent was put in reserve as a puppy saving fund for when they returned to their home in Washington State. The remaining 50 percent was used for discretionary purchases, often video games for sale on the local aftermarket and Snickers bars at the snack bar.

The business hit a rough patch when Spencer and Hannah, along with their parents, went home to Washington State on a three-month leave. They didn't want to lose their customer base while they were away, so they decided to turn the business over to two other children also living on the ship. Unfortunately, the new management was not nearly as diligent about the business as Spencer and Hannah. Service was intermittent: Some days the trash would not be picked up at all, with no notice or explanation. Many customers opted out of their weekly subscription and returned to carrying out their own garbage again. Among the customers who stayed, bill collection and revenue declined due to administrative oversights. Without an active manager like Spencer and without a One-Page Partnership Agreement, the business suffered greatly in the absence of its founders.

• • •

Who says you're just one person? You can hire an army of virtual assistants to do your bidding. You can carefully pursue partnerships with the goal of having $1 + 1 = 3$ or more. You can grow the business by reaching more prospects with the same message, or like Nathalie Lussier (the Raw Foods Witch), you can reach out to a whole different crowd while retaining your existing business.

Just don't open a sandwich shop with someone else's name on it. A better way is to franchise yourself.

KEY POINTS

- By leveraging skills and contacts, you can be in more than one place at the same time. Strategies to do this include outsourcing, affiliate recruitment, and partnerships.

- Use the hub-and-spoke model of maintaining one online home base while using other outposts to diversify yourself.

- When it comes to outsourcing, decide for yourself what's best. The decision will probably come down to two things: the kind of business you're building and your personality.

- Carefully chosen partnerships can create leverage; just make sure that's what you want to do. Use the One-Page Partnership Agreement for simple arrangements.

BECOME AS BIG AS *YOU* WANT TO BE (AND NO BIGGER).

> **"Nothing will work unless you do."**
> **—MAYA ANGELOU**

Among the people we've met in our story thus far, a few are active risk takers, charging ahead to storm the castle, career or finances be damned if they fail. But far more common are those who carefully take the time to build a business step by step. It's a myth that all those who choose to go it alone are Type A motorcycle riders, betting it all on the success or failure of one project. Entrepreneurs are not necessarily risk takers; it's just that they define risk and security differently from the way other people do.

Tsilli Pines, an Israeli-American designer who now lives in my hometown of Portland, Oregon, exemplifies the group of cautious entrepreneurs. Over the course of eight years, she crafted a business making *ketubot,* custom-designed Jewish wedding contracts. During most of that time, the business was a night-and-weekend project she worked on after coming home from the design studio where she was employed. With a regular paycheck from the day job, Tsilli felt safe experimenting with the business and learning as she went along. She also noticed an important side benefit to working this way: With limited hours to spend on the business, she had to make them count.

Thanks to referrals from happy couples, the business grew slowly but steadily, with more orders each year. Each *ketubah* was a labor of love, priced at $495. As 2009 drew to a close, Tsilli felt prepared to make the leap. She gave notice to her boss and colleagues and prepared to go full-time. This was it! She had jumped!

Except . . . the view on the other side wasn't all she had expected. The first week of freedom felt great; the second week she began to wonder, *What do I do all day?* "I underestimated the value of having some work that was collaborative and not self-directed," she said. Over the next few months, the business earned less than expected. Orders were still coming in and the situation was far from desperate, but Tsilli felt trapped, drained of the creativity she had thrived on while starting up.

"The all-or-nothing paradigm was too much pressure," she continued. "I'm running a creative business, but it's a creativity killer for me to define my whole income on the need to continuously deploy my creativity." It was a hard decision to make, but six months after leaving the design firm, she approached the owners with a proposal: How about coming back part-time? They said yes and were happy to have her.

Moving back to the studio three days a week was the right fit. When she had left six months earlier, she had a lot of responsibility as the lead designer; there was no way she could stick around in a lesser role without first leaving for a while. Coming back in under the radar gave her the security of having a certain amount of fixed income while retaining the freedom of working half-time on her other projects. Also, Tsilli now worked as a contractor instead of an employee, and that gave her an unexpected but important sense of still earning all her income "on her own," with roughly half coming from the studio and half from her business.

It was right for her to leave, and it was right to go back. The business is still profitable, but without the pressure of needing to rely on it exclusively. Tsilli summarizes it like this: "The feeling I have is that I'm still laying brick after brick. The different pieces interlock, and over time they may build to critical mass. But right now I'm in a good place."

The Choice

Tsilli's story illustrates the real challenge that befalls almost everyone with the opportunity to make a major career change and go it alone: finding a way to build systemization into the business, and deciding what role the business will play in the rest of their lives. Sooner or later, every successful business owner—accidental or otherwise—faces a choice: Where are we going with this thing? As described throughout the book, many of the members of our group made a deliberate decision to stay small, creating a "freedom business" for the purpose of having the freedom. Others chose to grow by carefully recruiting employees and going all in.

Here's how three people faced this critical choice, resolving it in different ways.

Option 1: Stay Small

No one is truly a born entrepreneur, but Cherie Ve Ard probably comes close. Working on her own since she was twenty, she's now thirty-eight and has never looked back. Her father was also an entrepreneur, starting the family software business that Cherie eventually took over. The company develops custom software solutions for health-care providers. In 2007 she hit the road with Chris Dunphy, her partner, and they traveled by RV across America. Being on the road while running a software company led to an obvious expansion: Cherie and Chris started a side business making mobile apps.

Business is good, but Cherie has purposely declined to pursue a number of expansion ideas. Here's how she puts it: "Without a doubt, the smartest decision I made was to set a specific intention to *not* grow the business. Growing up as the daughter of an entrepreneur, I watched my father's creativity and inventor mind-set get sapped as the business grew from just him to over fifty employees. The stress wore him down and diminished his quality of life."

When I last spoke to Cherie, she was on the island of Saint John, where she and Chris had settled in for a stay of a few months ("maybe longer, or as long as we feel like it"). Cherie earns a good income of at least $50,000 a year but is insistent that the money isn't the point. "My feeling of being a successful business owner is based on the quality of life I lead, not the amount of money I earn," she says. "I own my business. The business doesn't own me."

Option 2: Go Medium

In the SoDo area of downtown Seattle, a factory hums with the sound of sewing machines. Chinese-American women, many of whom have worked at the factory for years, diligently apply patches to backpacks and laptop bags. I tour the factory with Tom Bihn, the owner, and his business partner, Darcy Gray.

With more than twenty employees and his own factory, Tom isn't afraid of growth. But he turned his back on the biggest growth opportunity of all: distributing his popular bags through big-name retailers, many of which have asked repeatedly for partnerships. I was curious about this decision, so I sent Tom and Darcy an email later to ask for more input. Here's what they said:

> We chose to be our own manufacturer and direct retailer initially because it's more interesting. We get to march to our own drummer, so to speak. If the goal is simply to make money,

well, that's just boring. We wanted to make a cool business, with cool products, cool customers, and cool employees; we wanted to build a brand and a long-term place in the world. To sell to mass-market retailers may or may not be lucrative, but it does little for brand identity. It can also tie your fortune to a company over which you have no control: If they go down, you may go too. Our future is tied to what we do, decisions we make, and that's wicked good fun.

Marching to your own drummer is certainly interesting, and as Tom pointed out in another conversation, it may be a better business model as well. Cash flow for their business comes from many individual customers, so they never have to worry about one big store dropping their inventory (or defaulting on their debt). Because there's only one source, Tom Bihn bags are well positioned against being perceived as a commodity. Tom and Darcy are able to charge a good price for the bags and ensure that they can continue to support all the employees.

When asked about any bad days or negative experiences in the business, Tom said something I've been thinking about ever since: "All the bad days have two things in common: You know the right thing to do, but you let somebody talk you out of doing it."

At least in this case, Tom never let himself get talked out of what was clearly the right thing for him.

Option 3: Split the Difference

Sometimes the choice between small and big has more than two answers. A creative individual can learn her lessons about the wrong kind of growth and then apply them to the right kind. Meet Jessica Reagan Salzman, owner of a one-person bookkeeping shop in Attleboro, Massachusetts. I knew Jessica was a numbers person when she provided estimated income for the next year of exactly $110,899. Many entrepreneurs are lost in the bigger picture and aren't certain about their finances. They tended to answer my questions about income projections with statements like "Uh, about one hundred, maybe one-fifty or so." With Jessica, there was no need for follow-up.

Ironically, Jessica started the business after an unsettling experience at a new job she had just taken for a CPA. As she was settling into the job, she kept tallying figures and wondering why something wasn't balancing properly. She finally figured it out: Not only was the firm in trouble, it wouldn't have enough to pay her when the very first bookkeeping cycle came around. Oops. Jessica quit and decided to go it alone.

Right from the beginning, the business was profitable at a decent part-time level, and Jessica was focused on raising a family without worrying about making a ton of money. But one day, her husband, Michael, called and said he was coming home early. "That's nice," she said. "Any special occasion?" There was a pause before he told her the rest of the news: He had been laid off, effective immediately.

Jessica's business had been successful as a side project, but it didn't make nearly enough money to support a family, with their second child just three weeks old at that point. After the shock wore off, they talked about options, and Jessica decided to take the business to a higher level. Her husband became the primary caregiver at home, and Jessica went to work. The business quickly grew and all was well under the new arrangement, but then it started growing too fast. "We had made major progress in the direction of growing revenues," she said, "but we had also experienced soaring costs, and our bottom line clearly reflected the necessity for a major change.

"I just assumed that's what you were supposed to do," she continued. "As the business improves, you hire people. Right?" Unfortunately, although hiring people can sometimes help a business grow, it always creates much higher costs and fixed obligations. Jessica made more changes, switching her business to a sole proprietorship and returning to a one-woman shop.*

Don't Be a Firefighter: Work on Your Business

Regardless of which path you take, as your project grows in scope, you can find yourself spending all your time responding to things and little time actually creating anything. The solution to this common problem is to focus on working *on* your business as opposed to *in* it. When you're operating the business, you spend time putting out fires and keeping everything running as it should. Working on the business requires a higher-level approach.

Every morning, set aside forty-five minutes without Internet access. Devote this time exclusively to activities that improve your business—nothing that merely maintains the business. Think *forward motion* . . . What can you do to keep things moving ahead? Consider these areas:

BUSINESS DEVELOPMENT. This is work that grows the business. What new products or services are in the works? Are there any partnerships or joint ventures you're pursuing?

OFFER DEVELOPMENT. This kind of work involves using existing resources in a new way. Can you create a sale, launch event, or new offer to generate attention and income?

FIXING LONG-STANDING PROBLEMS. In every business, there are problems that creep up that you learn to work around instead of

---

*Jessica's business is called Heart Based Bookkeeping, and she likes to call herself a *soul* proprietor: someone who is emotionally and spiritually invested in her work.

Health Insurance

In the United States, it's the big question facing many prospective entrepreneurs: "How can I insure my family when I'm self-employed?" (Canadians and others can skip this section and breathe easy.) Unfortunately, universal health care is still a long way off before we catch up with the rest of the developed world.

To get some options, I surveyed our group of case studies (those from the U.S.) and also conducted several online conversations with large groups on Twitter and Facebook. The answers varied considerably. Someone wrote, "Get screwed and pay a lot of money for coverage that doesn't help you." Alas, in some cases, that statement may not be much of a stretch. But in other cases you have choices. Here are some of the most common ones.

Buy a high-deductible policy and pay cash for visits to the doctor. Perhaps the most common solution among the self-employed is to shop around and purchase a high-deductible policy to cover serious illness or accident. Then set aside a savings fund—either self-managed or with a health savings account (HSA)—to cover doctor's visits and preventive care. It's best to compare quotes from an independent broker, and in some cases a local or national group may offer a discounted policy. Several people mentioned the Freelancers Union, for example.*

Join a concierge program. A concierge program is the opposite of a high-deductible policy that covers only serious problems. For a monthly fee ($150 to 300 on average), you can visit the same doctor for most primary and preventive needs. You'll also get the doctor's email address and "call anytime" cell phone number, and the doctor will act as an

---

*See freelancersunion.org. Others mentioned eHealthInsurance.com and similar sites that offer an instant comparison of rates and plans for any state.

advocate and referrer if you need more serious care. Some people combine a concierge program with another policy to ensure that both short-term and disaster prevention needs are met.

Get insured through your partner. A number of business owners wrote to tell me that they relied on their spouse or partner's job to cover both of them while they worked full-time or part-time in the business. Courtney Carver was diagnosed with multiple sclerosis in 2006, and her medical bills would be $8,000 a month without insurance. "I feel fortunate that my husband works for a company that has group insurance," she says. "For now, starting a business together with him leaving his job is not an option because of my medical condition. We are looking at other out-of-state options for the future but are tied to his job for the insurance for now."

Of course, this option isn't available to you if you're single or if your partner doesn't have a job that provides insurance benefits, but if you do have the option, it may very well be the best one.

Stay on COBRA as long as possible. If you have lost your job, COBRA allows you to continue receiving the same health-care coverage for a certain length of time at the same price your former employer paid. You have to pay for it, but because it originally was based on a group rate, the cost is often lower (and coverage may be better) than that of any plan you could purchase yourself. Several people spoke of extending COBRA coverage for up to three years as they built their businesses.

Self-insure or use an HSA. "My health-care plan involves prayer, vitamins, and avoiding sharp objects," Amy Oscar told me on Twitter. Others explained that they were just being pragmatic about the poor options available to them, weighing the costs and what they perceived as limited benefits of an expensive plan they weren't likely to use. If you have a family or health-care issues, you may not be comfortable with this option.

addressing directly. Instead of perpetually ignoring these issues, use your non-firefighting time to deal with the root of the problem.

PRICING REVIEW. As discussed in Chapter 11, you should review your prices regularly to determine whether a price increase is in order. In addition, consider adding appropriate upsells, cross-sells, or other income-generating tools to your arsenal.

CUSTOMER COMMUNICATION. This involves not just dealing with emails or general inquiries, but initiating communication through newsletters and updates.

A key rule for all these activities is to initiate, not respond. Doing this for just forty-five minutes a day can bring huge rewards even when everything else is crazy and you spend the rest of the day putting out fires. Onward!

Monitoring Your Business

Regardless of your growth strategy, you'll want to pay attention to the health of your business. The best way to do this is with a two-pronged strategy:

Step 1: Select one or two metrics and be aware of them at any given time, focusing on sales, cash flow, or incoming leads.

Step 2: Leave everything else for a biweekly or monthly review where you delve into the overall business more carefully.

Some members of our group were much more diligent about tracking metrics than others, with a number of people talking about being obsessive over data and others saying they had "no idea" about what was happening in the business. (My opinion on this approach: Personalities and skill sets vary, but be wary of delegating all financial knowledge to someone else. Having no idea about money stuff is usually a bad sign.)

The metrics you want to track will vary with the kind of business. Here are a few of the most common examples.

Sales per day: How much money is coming in?

Visitors or leads per day: How many people are stopping by to take a look or signing up for more information?

Average order price: How much are people spending when they order?

Sales conversion rate: What percentage of visitors or leads become customers?

Net promoter score: What percentage of customers would refer your business to someone else?

Some businesses choose more specific metrics. Brandy Agerbeck, the graphic facilitator we met in Chapter 7, earns her living through corporate and non-profit bookings. Every year she needs a certain amount of bookings, so she keeps a set of index cards to track this number. When the index cards fill up, she knows she's good for a while and can focus on other things.

Once or twice a month it's good to take a deeper look at the business and record some metrics that should be improving over time. The kinds of things you'll probably be interested in are more detailed sales figures, site traffic and social media, and the growth of the business. You can get a free spreadsheet to help with this process in the online resources for this book at 100startup.com.

Built to Sell: Going *Really* Long

John Warrillow built and sold four companies before "retiring" to write, speak, and invest. After learning his lessons through those four experiences, he now advocates a specific model for owners of small companies who wish to sell their business one day. Most of John's recommendations relate to the need to create an actual company or organization that can thrive outside the business owners' specific skills.

In other words, the built-to-sell model is different from the model we've looked at in this book. Many of our case studies involve people who went into business for themselves because it was fun, not because they wanted to build something and then cash out. However, John's recommendations are solid for owners who want to pass a business on, and some of them can be adapted to improve a business even if you want to stick around. You can see how the two models compare in the table below.

BUILT TO SELL—$100 STARTUP COMPARISON

	Built to Sell	$100 Startup
Required capital	Variable but often high	Variable but usually low
Employees	Required	Optional
Freedom payoff	Big payday	No big payday
Secondary benefit	Build and move on	Do what you love

In trying to decide which path to pursue, the simple question to answer is: "What kind of freedom do you want?" John's model is all about creating an entity apart from yourself and then selling it for a big payday. The $100 Startup model is more about transitioning to a business or independent career that is based on something you love to do—in other words, something intrinsically related to the owner's skill or passion. Neither model is better; it just depends on your goals.

If you'd like to have the option of selling your business one day, John's point is that you have to plan for it by taking specific steps. The most important step in creating an independent identity for the business is to create a product or service with the potential to scale. This is an important distinction from many of the businesses we've described thus far, so let's take a look at how John explains it.

Teachable vs. Valuable Curve

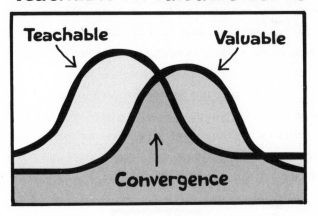

A scalable business is built on something that is both teachable and valuable. A CPA provides a highly valuable service, but it isn't easily teachable (she can't just bring someone into her practice and hand it over to him). On the other hand, you can teach someone how to bus tables at a restaurant in a few minutes, but that isn't a valuable service (lots of people can bus tables). Therefore, a business that has the potential to be sold easily for a high profit offers something at the intersection of teachable and valuable.

John built a subscription service that conducted financial research and provided a series of informative reports. This was highly valuable to his clients but also teachable to other employees. Another time he built a firm that produced consumer focus groups for big companies—again, a highly valuable service, but also replicable under new ownership.

• • •

The solutions found by Tsilli, Cherie, Tom, Jessica, and John varied considerably. In implementing their solutions, each of them said yes to something while saying no to something else. Tom declined to accept the deals from big-box retailers, but he wasn't afraid to hire employees and grow on his own terms. Cherie preferred to keep things small and intimate. Tsilli found security by growing her business *and* working as a contractor for her former employer.

What united these different experiences was a sense of controlling their own destiny and finding freedom in nurturing a meaningful project. As your own project grows, you'll also need to make decisions based on your preferences and specific vision. Just remember that these are good decisions to make and a good position to be in.

KEY POINTS

- There's more than one road to freedom, and some people find it through a combination of different working arrangements.

- "Going long" by pursuing growth and deciding to stay small are both acceptable options, and you can split the difference by "going medium." It all depends on what kind of freedom you'd like to achieve.

- Work "on" your business by devoting time every day to activities specifically related to improvement, not just by responding to everything else that is happening.

- Regularly monitor one or two key metrics that are the lifeblood of your business. Check up on the others monthly or bimonthly.

- A business that is scalable is both teachable and valuable. If you ever want to sell your business, you'll need to build teams and reduce owner dependency.

HOW TO SUCCEED EVEN IF
YOUR ROOF CAVES IN ON YOU.

**"Your time is limited, so don't waste it
living someone else's life."**
—STEVE JOBS

Almost everyone we've met in the book so far has some kind
of failure-to-success story. In many cases, the story is about
a product launch that fell flat, a partnership gone wrong, or the
loss of motivation for the wrong project. "I tried something and
it didn't work out . . . but then I moved on to something else" is a
common refrain. All these stories are valid and interesting, but I've
never heard a rise-from-the-ashes story quite as compelling as that
of John T. Unger, a sculpture artist from a small town in Michigan.
John's story is a tour de force of failure and fear that turned into
resilience and success.

As John tells it, the third best thing that ever happened to him
was having the roof of his studio collapse from under him while he
was standing on it, frantically trying to shovel snow. The building
was completely destroyed, and John spent the rest of the Michigan
winter alternating between shivering while he worked and warming
himself with an illegal unvented kerosene heater. It was a nightmare
scenario, but then a funny thing happened: The bank came out to

assess the damage and gave him a $10,000 commission. John used the commission as a down payment on two buildings he had been trying to purchase for a while. "I don't think the bank would have gone for the deal without the disaster," he says. "It forced them to take a real look at my business instead of them just thinking of me as another broke artist."

The second best thing that ever happened to John was losing his last day job as a graphic designer during the dot-com crash of 2000. The loss of the job led to the loss of everything else—his income, his girlfriend, his apartment, and even a piece of his thumb in an accident incurred while he was moving out of the apartment. While he was working the day job (seven days a week in 1999, seven days *total* in 2000), he also was working as much as ten hours a day on his art business.

After both of these experiences—losing the building and losing the day job—John was depressed and thought hard about what to do next. His friends advised him to suck it up and find work wherever he could, but in rural Michigan those days, John knew that there wasn't much work to be found. It was now or never, so he stuck with his goal and continued making progress.

The best thing that ever happened to John, as he tells the story, was a late-night disagreement with a crazed cab driver, who pulled him into the back room of a diner and held a gun to his head for a full ten minutes, screaming and threatening to pull the trigger. John finally escaped and walked out into another cold Michigan night, sweating, trembling, and glad to be alive. "I get it!" John yelled at the sky as he hobbled away. "I'm just so lucky!"

"You don't really worry about the small things after that," John says now. "Everything takes on a whole other level of meaning."

Unwanted Advice and Unneeded Permission

Much of this book contains various forms of advice, but don't confuse advice for permission. You don't need anyone to give you permission to pursue a dream. If you've been waiting to begin your own $100 startup (or anything else), stop waiting and begin. Charlie Pabst, a Seattle-based designer who left the corporate world to go it alone, said that the best thing he did was learn to ignore advice, even from friends who meant well. "My business and the life I lead now would never have happened had I not been obnoxiously stubborn to my own will," he said. "The fact is that the majority of people don't own their own businesses. And a certain percentage of that majority will not be happy or supportive about your exiting the nine-to-five world."

While usually well-meaning, unsolicited advice from people who think they know better can be unnecessary and distracting. Here's how Chelly Vitry, the founder of a Denver food tour business, puts it:

> The biggest lesson I learned was to trust my own judgment. When I started my tour business, I got all sorts of advice from people around me, ranging from why it wouldn't work at all to how things should be run on a day-to-day basis. I had researched it and knew it was a viable idea, so I decided to keep my own counsel and quit asking people what they thought.
>
> People who know less about the business than me do not get to make decisions about it. I value input, but now I seek it out from people who have unique perspectives about how I can improve.

Sometimes the best advice is none at all. If you know what you need to do, the next step is simply to do it. Stop waiting. Start taking action.

What Are We Afraid Of?

Toward the end of many follow-up discussions with most of the business owners profiled in the book, I asked about their biggest fears, worries, or concerns. All these people had been successful, earning at least $50,000 a year from their projects (many were earning much more), but what were they worried about? What kept them up at night?

Their concerns fit into two broad areas: external and internal. External concerns tended to relate to money and a changing marketplace. For example, a few businesses had been created to exploit imbalances in technology. These projects can be very profitable for a time, but when the music stops playing, the ride is over. A business that grows primarily from strong Google rankings or good placement in the iTunes store ("favored by the gods of Apple," as one person put it) is in danger of losing it all if fortunes change. Scott McMurren, who published the Alaska coupon books, said he was closely watching the online coupon craze, considering ways to update the business to be more digital-friendly.

The role of competition was mentioned frequently, although in very different ways. Several people said they weren't worried about what other businesses were doing, because they found it more productive to keep moving forward with their own original work. Others did worry, especially about building something unique only to see it copied or "stolen" by a more established company. Marianne Cascone, who makes children's clothing in a small partnership she runs with her cousin, illustrated this concern well:

> Our biggest fear, since the beginning, is that our products will be "knocked off" and our prices will be undercut. We are covered by patents and trademarks, but it still happens from time

to time. However, I am a firm believer that if I focus 100 percent on creating a quality product, we will rise to the top every time. We do not get sidetracked on other projects; we focus on keeping our customers extremely satisfied. There is still a chance that I will walk into Target and see my design on their shelf under another company's name. We are just hoping to have a place in that market so they are truly competing with us and not stealing from us.

Those who had expanded by hiring employees tended to worry about making sure they had enough cash flow and recurring income to keep the payroll going. If you own a solo shop and business tightens up, you may be able to tighten up along with it. But if you owe people a fixed amount of money on a fixed schedule, you can't do that. One business produced more than $2 million in annual revenue but earned only $60,000 in net income for the owner, in large part because of the high overhead of employing people and investing in infrastructure.

Holly Minch mentioned the Goldilocks principle: the idea that success is found within certain margins and not at the extremes. "I want the clients to get real value out of what we deliver," she said, "but not at the expense of our bottom line. And I want the team to have enough work to live well but not so much work that we're not living."

Others worried about "faking it" or needed to keep the wheels rolling after the initial passion faded away. "My biggest fear is that my consulting and writing becomes mediocre," said Alyson Stanfield in Colorado. "Success seems to be the ability to keep going, to keep the doors open," said Lee Williams-Demming in Costa Rica.

"Be careful of letting clients take your business in a direction that makes you hate your job," said Britta Alexander, one half of the husband-and-wife team running a marketing company in Hastings-on-Hudson, New York. "The further you go down that road, the harder it will be to correct course. And it's really hard to quit your job when it's your own company."

Digging deeper, the fears and worries were more closely related to issues of identity. "I love my work," someone said, "but what if I love only the work, or what if the thing I love is no longer fun because now it's all work?" Statements like these usually were followed by clarifying ones such as "Starting this business, no matter the eventual outcome, has been worth the energy, effort, and sacrifices it has taken thus far to get it off the ground."

One of our case studies, a Canadian manufacturer, said: "I used to be afraid to fail. I wanted concrete numbers telling me that we weren't going to lose before I took the leap. But if nobody was going to die, even in the absolute worst-case scenario, then what the hell was I so afraid of? I've never looked back."

A European designer was even more dramatic: "Do you want to know the honest truth? In the early days, I almost expected my business to be a failure. I believed that it had to be that way because it is the first business I have ever run, and I know the biggest successes have the biggest failures behind them. It sounds perverse but I almost wanted it to fail so I could look back and say, 'Yep, that one failed, but I learned from it!'" (Fortunately or not, his business is doing just fine.)

The Moment They Knew

As I reviewed thousands of pages of survey data and made countless follow-up calls, I learned to ask people if the decision to start their business had been worth it. You might think that such a question is simplistic; wouldn't most responses be "yes"? Well, perhaps . . . but one of the best parts of the study was hearing exactly how a group of diverse people answered this question. There was usually a story behind the affirmative answer, and the story often related to a particular day, event, or moment when they knew their business was going to work. As we come to the end of this journey, I thought you should hear from a few of them directly.

Gary Leff
Book Your Award
Fairfax, Virginia

I never thought that people would pay for the service that I offer, so the very first time I received a check in payment for services from my very first client, it hit me like a ton of bricks—there's real money on the table here! And when I saw a letter from that very first customer published in a magazine recommending my service, I realized that there was both appreciation and demand for what I was offering.

Karen Starr
Hazel Tree Interiors
Akron, Ohio

Even with our excellent credit history, 2010 was a bad time in banking to ask for money. We didn't need much, but we couldn't swing it completely on our own. My husband Jon and I needed a small credit line to lease the building where we planned to house our interior design and framing business. Unfortunately, the bank said no.

Later that day, Jon was on the phone with the landlord of the building, telling him that we just weren't going to be able to make it work and that he could release the building to the other interested party. As I heard him saying those words on the phone, I had an incredible surge of hope, and I remember shouting, "Jon, no! We have to give it another shot! Tell him we just need a few more days to try again. We'll have to go back in to the bank and make them hear us out. If they'll just sit down and listen, they will believe in us."

It totally worked! The bank did hear our plea, and we eventually got what we needed to get going. Two years in, and we couldn't be more thrilled. But we almost accepted the fact that it wasn't meant to be and carried on with our lives. I am so glad we put in more effort. It meant everything to us to give it one more passionate plea.

David Fugate
LaunchBooks Literary Agency
Encinitas, California

For me it was when I signed a big client after flying out to their corporate offices, making a pitch, and getting a tour of the grounds. When I got the call from his marketing VP that they wanted to go with me over a couple other agents they had met, that was the moment when I knew LaunchBooks was going to work. Truth be told, I didn't even know that I had any doubts about it working before that call, because I had been an agent for more than twelve years already and knew what I was doing. But because of the way my employment worked at the old agency, I literally had to leave with nothing—no income stream whatsoever from the 1,000 books I had sold while I was there—so I was literally starting from scratch. But when I got that call, I had this enormous feeling of relief and excitement wash over me, and I just absolutely knew it was going to work.

The funny thing was that the client ended up being an unbelievable jerk and pulled out of his book deal over repeated problems with the publisher. He didn't like a mock cover that they put together and their preference that he actually follow the proposal we had sent them for the content, so rather than trying to work anything out, he just decided the publisher "didn't get it" and pulled out. Then a little while later he had his assistant send me a termination letter without so much as a conversation, even though I had managed to generate a decent offer for what was a brutally difficult book to sell.

It didn't matter, though. I still had that first moment on the phone and never looked back. I've since been on my own and selling books for more than ten years.

Kyle Hepp
Independent Photographer
Santiago, Chile

My husband and I were traveling around Europe after I had been hit by a car. We were going to travel and then go back to Chile to shoot weddings until the bookings stopped coming in and then go back to having "normal" jobs. We had been CouchSurfing to try and save money, but after a month and a half on the road I was sick of it. So we decided to splurge in Italy. We checked into an amazing room at the Meridien, and I decided to pay an ungodly amount to use the Internet for ten minutes. And that was when I saw the email. It would be our second U.S. wedding and our first wedding where I had quoted more than simply travel costs. The bride had decided to hire us, and she was going with our biggest package, over $5,000.

I freaked out. I called my mom and then I called my dad,

screaming—stupidly using the hotel phone, which ended up costing another hundred bucks. I should've paid for another ten minutes of the internet and used Skype. I wasn't freaking out because of the money, though. It was because for a bride to pay that amount of money to photographers who don't even live in her country requires a huge leap of faith. And that was when I realized that if there was one bride willing to hire us and fly us in, there were probably more. And I started to think that if we could work both in Chile and outside of Chile, we could make this work. So we did.

Jonathan Pincas
The Tapas Lunch Company
Spain and Norwich, United Kingdom

The big day for us was August 20, 2008, also known as the day when we realized our dream of moving back to my partner's native Spain. When we set up the company in England in 2005, it was with the aim of eventually being able to move back to Spain and run the business remotely, although we weren't sure how long this would take. We had set up a perfect infrastructure, with cloud-based business management software, VoIP telephones, and so on, but the logistics of outsourcing was proving the biggest hurdle. We couldn't find a company that could deal with the complexity of 250 different products, most of which were labeled in Spanish.

When we finally managed to set up the contracted logistics operation and drove away from the warehouse knowing that we no longer had to do all the shipping ourselves and that the following day we were getting on a boat to Spain, I knew we had achieved what we set out to do.

• • •

As I traveled the world meeting our group of unexpected entrepreneurs, I heard story after story like these. Over and over, they
echoed a similar theme: When you have these moments, hold on
to them. They provide encouragement and positive reinforcement
when times are hard.

The $100 Recap

Before we close it out, let's look back at the key lessons of this
book. First and most important, the quest for personal freedom
lies in the pursuit of value for others. Get this right from the
beginning and the rest will be much easier. Always ask, "How can
I help people more?"

Borrowing money to start a business, or going into debt at all, is
now completely optional. Like many of the people you met in this
book, you can start your own microbusiness for $100 or less.

Focus relentlessly on the point of convergence between what
you love to do and what other people are willing to pay for. Remember that most core needs are emotional: We want to be loved and
affirmed. Relate your product or service to attractive benefits, not
boring features.

If you're good at one thing, you're probably good at something
else. Use the process of skill transformation to think about all the
things you're good at, not just the obvious ones.

Find out what people want, and find a way to give it to them.
Give them the fish!

There is no consulting school. You can set up shop and charge
for specialized help immediately. (Just remember to offer something specific and provide an easy way to get paid.)

Some business models are easier than others to start on a budget. Unless you have a compelling reason to do something different, think about how you can participate in the knowledge economy.

Action beats planning. Use the One-Page Business Plan and other quick-start guides to get under way without waiting.

Crafting an offer, hustling, and producing a launch event will generate much greater results than simply releasing your product or service to the world with no fanfare.

The first $1.26 is the hardest, so find a way to get your first sale as quickly as possible. Then work on improving the things that are working, while ignoring the things that aren't.

By "franchising yourself" through partnerships, outsourcing, or creating a different business, you can be in more than one place at the same time.

Decide for yourself what kind of business you'd like to build. There's nothing wrong with deliberately staying small (many of the subjects of our stories did exactly that) *or* scaling up in the right way.

It only gets better as you go along.

• • •

When we last left off, Jamestown Coffee Company was opening for business in Lexington, South Carolina. Owner James Kirk had moved south from Seattle and kicked things off. What happened next? Did a flood of loyal visitors show up right away?

Not exactly. It was a tough start, settling into a community not familiar with specialty coffee. The shop grew one customer at a time, with a focus on providing personal experiences and encouraging repeat business. One weekend, James and his crew gave out coupons for a free coffee at a local golf tournament. A man stopped in to redeem his coupon and mentioned that he normally picked up his morning cup at the gas station but was inspired to try something new. The next day he returned, saying it was the best cup of coffee he had ever had.

A morning group began to gather most weekdays, consisting of regulars from all kinds of backgrounds—a lawyer, a clergyman, a computer guy, a mechanic. People who used to buy instant coffee at the grocery store began making a special trip every week to pick up the superior stuff at Jamestown Coffee Company. Slowly but surely, the business stabilized.

James thought back on the discouragement he had received from well-meaning friends when he first told them about moving down south. "You can't start a business during a recession," they said. "You can't move across the country without a job." "Most small businesses fail within one year." "Almost all mom and pop restaurants fail within the first year." On and on it went. And every time someone gave him a reason he couldn't succeed in what he had set out to do, he made another note in his "non-planning" folder: merely one more obstacle to overcome.

Elsewhere, Jen and Omar continued making their maps in Columbus, Ohio, expanding to wholesale accounts in addition to the direct sales with which they started. They were featured recently in an Expedia commercial and are thinking about opening up a boutique travel store as part of the next adventure.

Karol Gajda and Adam Baker produced two other mega-sales, each one bringing in a six-figure payday for themselves and their affiliates. I asked for their help in producing the launch for this book just as soon as they finished carrying the bags of cash to the bank.

Brandon Pearce was planning a family move to Malaysia. The business now brings in over $50,000 a month.

Benny Lewis was still language hacking his way around the world, moving to Istanbul for a crash course in Turkish. Next up: a planned attempt at learning Mandarin Chinese in Taiwan.

The Mondo Beyondo course started by Andrea Scher and Jen Lemen has served more than five thousand participants, producing $500,000 in revenue for the two partners.

Brett Kelly's $120,000 e-book has become a $160,000 e-book. His wife continues to stay at home with the kids, and they are now completely debt-free.

Perhaps the most important lesson arrived in an email from Emily Cavalier, who had recently left a high-paying job in Manhattan to pursue Mouth of the Border, a tour and events business focused on ethnic foods. I asked how often she still felt motivated to go it alone, and she told me: "Every single day. The greatest benefit has been going to bed just as excited as if not more excited than when I woke up. I get to work day in, day out on something that fully engages me and elicits not just my passions but the passion of tons of other people, too."

Yes, like Emily and everyone else in this book, you can do this too. You aren't alone out there.

Sure, you can learn through failure, and most likely you'll have at least one false start on the road to freedom. But failure is overrated—who says you'll fail? You can just as easily succeed. You can apply the lessons from these stories and create the new life you want.

Ready?

KEY POINTS

- Advice can be helpful, but you can also just step out and take a big leap. Don't wait for someone to give you permission.

- More than competition or other external factors, the biggest battle is against our own fear and inertia. Thankfully, this also means we are in complete control of managing it.

- When you have a success or "moment you knew" story, hold on to it; these experiences are powerful and will help you later if times get hard.

- The most important lesson in the whole book: Don't waste your time living someone else's life.

CODA

The story about freedom and value doesn't end in the Western world; these themes are just as important in helping people create opportunities for themselves wherever they are. In many parts of Africa and Asia, more people work as buyers and sellers in the informal economy than work as employees for someone else. They may not all be professional bloggers or mobile application developers (yet), but they earn their living through the principles outlined in this book.

In Phnom Penh, Cambodia, I met a tuk-tuk driver named Rhett. Tuk-tuks are the open-air taxis of Southeast Asia in which you can ride anywhere in the city for a dollar or two. Some tuk-tuk drivers, just like some cab drivers in other places around the world, are unreliable and dishonest. Rhett, however, is both reliable and honest, always arriving early to pick up a passenger and sometimes delivering regular customers to their destinations at no charge.

Most tuk-tuk drivers in Cambodia make just $2 to $5 a day, but Rhett earns up to $50 a day. He does this through a combination of hard work and careful strategy. The hard work comes by not sleeping or gambling the afternoon away as many of his colleagues do. The strategy lies in understanding that he is better off by serving regular clients instead of constantly roaming the streets looking for one-time fares. While I was in town visiting a friend, Rhett made it clear that he was at my service, giving me his mobile number and telling me to call him "day and night."

After his core business model of serving regulars was established, Rhett created "multiple streams of income" by adding a sign for a popular bakery on the back of his tuk-tuk. The bakery pays him a fixed amount each month, plus a small commission for any business he brings in. He also regularly asks his customers for referrals and testimonials to increase his client base. If a customer needs help getting to a destination outside of Phnom Penh, Rhett will find a taxi or bus driver available for hire, making sure he is honest and then following up with the customer after the trip to confirm that all went well.

He does all of this while speaking only limited English ("I practice every day, but my tongue becomes tired," he told me) and without any formal education at all. Some of the extra money he earns goes to a savings fund, a safety net almost no other tuk-tuk driver has. His daughter is now in college, the first in their family to finish high school.

As you work to improve your own circumstances, with freedom as the goal and value as the currency that gets you there, consider how these principles apply elsewhere. I like Rhett's story because it shows that creativity and initiative will get you far, regardless of the starting point. In many parts of the world, however, the starting point is much farther away than it is for most readers of this book. Starting a business in the developing world is often a difficult, highly bureaucratic endeavor—which is why so many people like Rhett operate in the informal sector. In some of these places, millions of people still lack access to clean water and other basic needs.

In my own business and writing career, I invest at least 10 percent of all revenue with organizations that make better improvements around the world than I could make on my own. (This includes the royalties for this book, so if you've purchased it, thanks for the help.) I don't consider this investment a charitable act; I consider it a natural response to the fact that I've been more fortunate than others.

While creating freedom for yourself, how can you be part of a global revolution to increase opportunity for everyone? If you're not sure, you can join the $100 Startup community in our campaign for clean water in Ethiopia by visiting charitywater.org/aonc. You can also sign up with groups, such as Kiva.org and AcumenFund .org, that provide loans (usually very small ones) to help people start microbusinesses in their own communities.

Of course, these answers aren't the only ones. If you have a better answer or just a different one, work on that instead. Pursue your dream of freedom wherever it leads . . . while also thinking about how it can intersect with creating more opportunities for people like Rhett.

DISCLOSURES AND INTERESTING FACTS

No business exists in a vacuum, and many of the stories told here will evolve over time. Financial information was supplied to me by those in the case studies and was current at the time of printing. We did our best to ensure accuracy with repeated fact checking and verification, but any errors are mine.

My wife, Jolie, teaches at the Happy Knits store profiled in Chapter 12. She is also responsible for several other leads to craft businesses. Jonathan Fields (Chapter 7) and Tsilli Pines (Chapter 13) are longtime friends.

I was offered samples by some of the businesses mentioned in the study. Accepted: a bottle of California Syrah from Verge Wine, blog promotion from Evernote, and a free Empire Builder bag from Tom Bihn. Declined: a jar of mustard from Sono Trading and a free Excel template from Mr. Spreadsheet.

When I wasn't roaming the world conducting interviews, much of this book was written in the following Portland cafés: Rocking Frog, Albina Press, Crema, Stumptown, and Starbucks on 37th and Hawthorne. Most popular order at the Rocking Frog: hot cinnamon donut and 12-ounce Americano.

Number of times the phrases *"cha-ching!"* and *"woop-woop"* were removed from the manuscript during copyedits: eight.

John T. Unger (Chapter 14) has revised his list of the best things that ever happened to him. He now puts meeting his wife, Marcie, another artist, at the very top of the list. They live and work in a new studio with a much sturdier roof.

When next in Cambodia, you can hire Rhett the tuk-tuk driver by calling +855 12 543 767.

BUT WAIT, THERE'S MORE!

All good things come to an end, and if you've read this far, I hope it's been a good use of your time. If you'd like more, head over to 100startup.com, where you'll find a community of other readers, unexpected entrepreneurs, and people from different backgrounds all planning their escape to a life of their own making.

In addition to all the customizable exercises from the book (the Instant Consultant Biz, the One-Page Promotion Plan, and so on), you'll get a number of resources that didn't make it in the final version:

- Data and sample interviews from the study, including transcripts and audio files
- Video interviews with Benny Lewis (Chapter 4), Jen and Omar (Chapter 6), and Karol Gajda (Chapter 8)
- Economics of blog subscribers, where you'll see how much money an average blogger earns
- More analysis on subscription payments, upsells, and pricing structures you can use to ramp up your income
- The two words all business owners can say to set themselves up for an unlimited series of long-term product launches

And as they say, so much more! All of this info is *free*, and you don't need to register to receive it. We also have a community forum and additional resources for sale, including more case studies and specific business strategies. Join us at 100startup.com.

Finally, if you enjoyed the book, feel free to let me know. You can write in directly from chrisguillebeau.com, where I follow the model outlined in several of the case studies in this book, publishing at least 80 percent of my writing and business work on a regular basis for free.

twitter.com/chrisguillebeau
facebook.com/artofnonconformity

FISH STORIES APPENDIX

Twenty-Five Selected Case Studies

In Chapter 2, we met Barbara and John Varian, owners of the V6 Ranch in California. Barbara could have described her business in a typical fashion: "We have a ranch. People pay to visit and ride horses." Instead, she said something much more powerful: "We help our guests become someone else, even if just for a day. Come stay with us and you'll be a cowboy." The difference between these two statements is huge! The first statement is merely descriptive, whereas the second evokes a powerful, emotional connection.

Like the V6 Ranch, every business has a way to describe itself in a traditional (i.e., boring) way and at least one much sexier way that stimulates a better response. There are two keys to remember in figuring out the difference for your own project:

1. Give people what they really want. Give them the fish!
2. Sell emotional benefits ("Be a cowboy") instead of descriptive features ("Ride horses").

Here are twenty-five people from the study, all of whom found ways to differentiate between something merely descriptive and something that evokes a more passionate response.

Name	Business	Fact-Based Description	Emotion-Based Promise
JASON GLASPEY	Paleo Plan	Weekly diet and recipe planning guide	*Take control of your health by eating naturally (and leave the details to us).*
BROOKE THOMAS	Practice Abundance	Course on running a wellness practice	*Increase profits while running a smoother, more streamlined clinic.*
PURNA DUGGIRALA	Spreadsheet templates	Templates to help frequent users of Microsoft Excel	*Become an office superhero: Help your colleagues and get your work done quickly.*
SELENA CUFFE	Heritage Link Brands	Wine imported from South Africa	*Drink great wine and feel good about supporting minority-owned vineyards.*
PATRICK MCCRANN	Endurance Nation	Group triathlon training	*You're not alone! Join a supportive community of amateur athletes.*
BRANDY AGERBECK	Graphic facilitation	Visual documentation of meetings	*Capture your group's big ideas in a fun way that will ensure a long-term impact.*
HEATHER ALLARD	The Mogul Mom	Resources for "mom entrepreneurs"	*Stay home with your kids and earn a good income without going into debt.*
JONATHAN PINCAS	Tapas Lunch Company	UK-based importer of Spanish foods	*Viva España! Celebrate the Mediterranean lifestyle without leaving home.*
REESE SPYKERMAN	Design by Reese	Website and graphic design	*Your brand is more than a website. We'll help you tell a story that communicates your core mission.*
MICHAEL TRAINER	Reckoning Studios	Media production	*We'll document your organization's mission in a short, professionally produced video.*
ALYSON STANFIELD	Stanfield Art Associates	Consulting for artists	*Attention, artists: Get paid to make the art you love. I'll show you how.*
ELIZABETH MACCRELLISH	Squam Art Workshops	Weekend retreats for artists and crafters	*Make art in a beautiful lakeside setting with an intimate group of friends.*
JESSICA REAGAN SALZMAN	Heart Based Bookkeeping	Bookkeeping and tax preparation services	*I'll worry about your money stuff so you can spend time running your business.*

Name	Business	Fact-Based Description	Emotion-Based Promise
KAREN STARR	Hazel Tree Interiors	Interior design services	*Make your home a restful sanctuary, a place your whole family enjoys.*
SARAH YOUNG	Happy Knits	Retail shop that sells yarn	*Knitting is fun! Come in to learn, restock, knit, or just hang out.*
ERICA COSMINSKY	The Small Business Transcriptionist	Service provider that transcribes calls and meetings	*Capture important information that your customers will value, with basic formatting and layout included at no additional charge.*
AKIRA MORITA	Design Kompany	Regional leader in design services	*You'll get the best service from our family-owned shop, and we won't finish until you're 100 percent satisfied.*
DAVID WACHTENDONK	Murder Mystery Maniacs	Group event planner	*Leave the party planning to us. We'll bring a fun experience to your group or organization.*
EMILY CAVALIER	Mouth of the Border	Ethnic food reviews and "midnight brunch" group experience	*Have fun, eat good food, and spend time with friends during a unique evening.*
RIDLON KIPHART	Live Adventurously	Group tours to exotic destinations	*Live adventurously by joining us for the trip of a lifetime.*
KRISTIN MCNAMARA	SLO Op Climbing	Community gym and climbing center	*Learn a new, challenging skill in a safe, community-centered environment.*
SCOTT MCMURREN	Alaska TourSaver	Coupon books for independent visitors to Alaska	*You'll recoup your entire investment by using just one of our coupons— leaving you with 200 more to get the best possible discounts.*
JEN LEMEN	Mondo Beyondo	Online life planning course	*Learn to turn big dreams into reality in a fun, closed environment with other women.*
JEN ADRION	These Are Things	Online store that sells maps	*Our maps will help you remember where you've been and dream of where you're going.*
CODY LIMBAUGH	PXTFitness	Personal training and exercise plans	*Want to get in shape but keep falling off the wagon? I'll help . . . and it will actually be fun.*

Note: Some of these businesses are operated by co-owners or another form of partnership. To simplify, I've listed the primary contact I talked with during my research.

GRATITUDE

There's an old saying about the combined knowledge of the pope and a peasant being greater than the knowledge of only the pope. In this case, I felt like the peasant learning from one hundred popes. After a decade of fumbling along, I know how to operate my own business, but crafting a narrative around the lessons of so many other people required me to learn much more than I could contribute by myself.

The hundred-plus case studies I focused on for the final draft (as well as the 1,400 other people who submitted stories and info) deserve my greatest thanks. They were patient with my numerous surveys, requests for additional info, and continual follow-ups. Being willing to share financial information about their business was especially generous. I had planned to gently push for access to finances if needed, but in most cases I didn't have to push—almost everyone was willing and open to share whatever information would help others.

I do most of my other writing without access to an outside editor, a situation which has numerous advantages, but also a key disadvantage: Sometimes I get tired and take the easy way out. Fortunately, that strategy wasn't an option here, all thanks to Rick Horgan, leader of the Crown team that published the book. Rick worked diligently and held my feet to the fire time after time, making for a much better finished product. I'm also grateful to Tina Constable and everyone else at Crown, and to my tireless literary agent, David Fugate.

Dave Navarro first gave me the analogy of a product launch being like a Hollywood movie. Jason Fried was the first person I heard say "Failure is overrated." I've undoubtedly borrowed other concepts and ideas, so if I've stolen your idea, consider it an act of unintentional flattery.

I continue to learn every day from Seth Godin, Chris Brogan, friends and colleagues in the *LifeRemix* network, Scott Harrison, Gary Parker, and Susan Parker.

Jolie Guillebeau, my wife and chief proofreader, patiently endured repeated discussions about hustling and bad franchises. Many sections of the book were greatly improved thanks to her insight. Critical readings of the text were further accompanied by my four-pawed assistant Libby (aka "The Liberator"). Libby is also responsible for moderating comments on my blog—a tough job for someone who sleeps approximately twenty-two hours a day.

Wherever I go, I work closely with Reese Spykerman, superstar designer, and Nicky Hajal, genius developer. On this project, I'm also grateful for the collaboration with Mike Rohde, who made the fun illustrations you can see throughout this book. Special thanks to Stephanie D. Zito for last-minute cover-art consultation.

Every summer, the World Domination Summit action team puts on a weekend adventure like no other, and I'm thrilled to be along for the ride. All of my work is for and sustained by the AONC community, which greatly inspires me with their stories of change and adventure.

Finally, I offer my appreciation and gratitude to you, the reader. I hope you found these pages worthwhile. Feel free to let me know about your own search for freedom and value by writing in from chrisguillebeau.com or saying hi on Twitter (@chrisguillebeau).

Chris Guillebeau
Portland, Oregon

ROCKSTARS FROM *THE $100 STARTUP*

Name	Business	Location	Industry
MICHAEL HANNA	*Mattress Lot*	Portland, OR	Furniture
SARAH YOUNG	*Happy Knits*	Portland, OR	Bricks and mortar
SUSANNAH CONWAY	*Photographer + Instructor*	Bath, UK	Education and photography
BENNY LEWIS	*Fluent in 3 Months*	No fixed address	Independent publisher
MEGAN HUNT	*Custom dresses*	Omaha, NE	Bridal design and shared work/ Co-working space
JESSICA REAGAN SALZMAN	*Heart Based Bookkeeping*	Attleboro, MA	Bookkeeping
TARA GENTILE	*Scoutie Girl*	Wyomissing, PA	Independent publisher
DAVID HENZELL	*Lightbulb Design*	West Yorkshire, UK	Branding and design
ERICA COSMINSKY	*Small business transcriptionist*	Nashville, TN	Service provider
TOM BIHN	*Tom Bihn*	Seattle, WA	Bag manufacturer
OMAR NOORY	*These Are Things*	Columbus, OH	Gifts and novelty items
JEN ADRION	*These Are Things*	Columbus, OH	Gifts and novelty items
PATRICK MCCRANN	*Endurance Nation*	Boston, MA	Fitness
CHARLIE PABST	*Charfish Design*	Seattle, WA	Design services
JEREMY BROWN	*No Limit Publishing*	Tempe, AZ	Service provider
KAT ALDER	*WildKat PR*	London, UK	Public relations
JADEN HAIR	*Steamy Kitchen*	Tampa, FL	Food advice

Name	Business	Location	Industry
BRANDON PEARCE	*Music Teacher's Helper*	Costa Rica	Independent publisher
SCOTT AND JOHN MEYER	*9 Clouds*	Brookings, SD	Media and business consulting
JAMES KIRK	*Jamestown Coffee Company*	Columbia, SC	Coffee shop
BARBARA VARIAN	*V6 Ranch*	Parkfield, CA	Cowboy ranch
KELLY NEWSOME	*Higher Ground Yoga*	Washington, DC	Yoga practice
KYLE HEPP	*Kyle Hepp Photography*	Santiago, Chile	Photography
PURNA DUGGIRALA	*Chandoo.org*	India	Consultant
BROOKE SNOW	*Brooke Snow Fine Arts*	Smithfield, UT	Educator
GARY LEFF	*Book Your Award*	Washington, DC	Travel consulting
MIGNON FOGARTY	*QDT network*	Reno, NV	Broadcasting
GABRIELLA REDDING	*Hoopnotica*	Venice, CA	Hula hoop manufacturer
ZACH NEGIN	*SoNo Trading Company*	San Diego, CA	Gourmet food
BERNARD VUKAS	*Mr. Spreadsheet*	No fixed address	Web development
JACK COVERT	*800-CEO-READ*	Milwaukee, WI	Book distributor
JEN LEMEN	*Mondo Beyondo*	Silver Spring, MD	Independent publisher
DARREN ROWSE	*ProBlogger*	Melbourne, Australia	Digital photography
BRIAN CLARK	*Copyblogger*	Dallas, TX	Online services
BRETT KELLY	*Evernote Essentials*	Fullerton, CA	Independent publisher
MARK RITZ	*Kinetic Koffee Company*	Arcata, CA	Coffee roaster
KRIS MURRAY	*Day-care marketing*	Hudson, OH	Service provider
RIDLON "SHARKMAN" KIPHART	*Live Adventurously*	No fixed address	Adventure travel
JASON GLASPEY	*Paleo Plan*	Portland, OR	Independent publisher
AMY TURN SHARP	*Little Alouette*	Columbus, OH	Toy manufacturer
NICHOLAS LUFF	*Independent consultant*	Vancouver, BC	Business consulting
MICHAEL TRAINER	*Global Poverty Project*	New York City	Media
NICK GATENS	*Photographer*	Louisville, KY	Photography
SELENA CUFFE	*Heritage Link Brands*	Los Angeles, CA	Food and wine
DANIEL NISSIMYAN	*Matix Ltd.*	Kiryat Shmona, Israel	Service provider

Name	Business	Location	Industry
SCOTT MCMURREN	*Alaska TravelGram*	Anchorage, AL	Travel discount provider
JONATHAN FIELDS	*Sonic Yoga*	New York City	Yoga studio
BRANDY AGERBECK	*Loosetooth*	Chicago, IL	Graphic facilitator
NEV LAPWOOD	*Snowboard Addiction*	Whistler, BC	Online education
KAROL GAJDA	*Only 72*	Austin, TX	Independent publisher
ADAM BAKER	*Only 72*	Indianapolis, IN	Independent publisher
DAVID WACHTENDONK	*Murder Mystery Maniacs*	Chicago, IL	Event planning
ANDREAS KAMBANIS	*London Cyclist*	London, UK	Independent publisher
ELIZABETH MACCRELLISH	*Squam Art Workshops*	New Hampshire	Event planning
HEATHER ALLARD	*The Mogul Mom*	Providence, RI	Consultant and coach
KAREN STARR	*Hazel Tree Interiors*	Akron, OH	Interior design
ALYSON STANFIELD	*Stanfield Art Associates*	Golden, CO	Art consulting
JOHN MOREFIELD	*The 5-Cent Architect*	Seattle, WA	Architecture
DEREK SIVERS	*MuckWork*	Singapore	Services for musicians
NAOMI DUNFORD	*IttyBiz*	London, ON	Marketing consultant
SHANNON OKEY	*Cooperative Press*	Cleveland, OH	Hobbyist and publisher
CHELLY VITRY	*Denver Gourmet Tours*	Denver, CO	Tours
CHERIE VE ARD	*Two Steps Beyond*	No fixed address	Web development
EMMA REYNOLDS	*e3 Reloaded*	Hong Kong	Global consultancy
KRISTIN MCNAMARA	*SLO Op Climbing*	San Luis Obispo, CA	Fitness
PERRY MARSHALL	*Consulting*	Chicago, IL	Advertising consulting
REESE SPYKERMAN	*Design by Reese*	No fixed address	Design services
ANDY DUNN	*Luibh and Infinite Touch*	Ireland	Design and development
NATHALIE LUSSIER	*Raw Foods Witch*	Toronto, ON	Consultant
BROOKE THOMAS	*The Well Practice*	New Haven, CT	Health practitioner
NYANI QUARMYNE	*Photographer*	Ghana	Photography

RALF HILDEBRANDT	*Avano AG*	Stuttgart, Germany	Sales consultancy
JAMILA TAZEWELL	*11:11 Enterprises*	Los Angeles, CA	Gifts and novelty items
JONATHAN PINCAS	*Tapas Lunch Company*	Spain	Food importing
ADAM WESTBROOK	*Studio.fu*	London, UK	Design services
LEE WILLIAMS-DEMMING	*Tropical House Interiors*	Costa Rica	Furniture importing
ELEANOR MAYRHOFER	*e.m.papers*	Munich, Germany	Paper products
SPENCER COPLEY	*Copley Trash Services*	West Africa	Service provider
TSILLI PINES	*New Ketubah*	Portland, OR	Judaic art and weddings
COURTNEY CARVER	*Be More with Less*	Salt Lake City, UT	Consultant
JOHN WARRILLOW	*Built to Sell*	Toronto, ON	Consultant
JOHN T. UNGER	*Independent artist*	Mancelona, MI	Sculpture artist
MARIANNE CASCONE	*Bon Bon Cupcakes*	Kansas City, MO	Children's clothing
HOLLY MINCH	*LightBox Collaborative*	San Francisco, CA	Design services
BRITTA ALEXANDER	*Eat Media*	Hastings-on-Hudson, NY	Media
DAVID FUGATE	*LaunchBooks*	Encinitas, CA	Literary agency
EMILY CAVALIER	*Mouth of the Border*	New York City	Food and wine

Notes: "No fixed address" means that this person operates his or her business while traveling the world. Some businesses are run by multiple partners. The names listed here are the ones I spoke with for the study.

INDEX